D1647729

# SEVEN SNARES OF THE ENEMY

# SEVEN SNARES OF THE ENEMY

## BREAKING FREE FROM THE DEVIL'S GRIP

## ERWIN W. LUTZER

**MOODY PRESS**
CHICAGO

© 2001 by
ERWIN W. LUTZER

All rights reserved. No part of this book may be reproduced in any form without permission in writing from the publisher, except in the case of brief quotations embodied in critical articles or reviews.

All Scripture quotations, unless otherwise indicated, are taken from the *Holy Bible, New International Version*®. NIV®. Copyright © 1973, 1978, 1984 by International Bible Society. Used by permission of Zondervan Publishing House. All rights reserved.

Scripture quotations marked NASB are taken from the *New American Standard Bible*®, © Copyright The Lockman Foundation 1960, 1962, 1963, 1968, 1971, 1972, 1973, 1975, 1977, 1995. Used by permission.

Scripture quotations marked KJV are taken from the King James Version.

Library of Congress Cataloging-in-Publication Data

Lutzer, Erwin W.
    Seven snares of the Enemy : breaking free from the Devil's grip / Erwin W. Lutzer.
       p. cm.
    Includes bibliographical references.
    ISBN 0-8024-1164-9
    1. Christian life. 2. Sins. I. Title.

BV4501.3 .L876 2001
248.4--dc21

00-51545


1 3 5 7 9 10 8 6 4 2

*Printed in the United States of America*

# CONTENTS

# FROM
# MY HEART
# TO YOURS

We must humbly admit that a single decision can trip a series of dominoes that will destroy the rest of our lives. And although God's forgiveness is available, the consequences of our foolish choice can dog us for years to come. And, yes, our failures might have repercussions for all of eternity. Look around us, and we all know people who have had normal lives gone bad. Some of them have lost in a moment what it took years for them to build and protect.

What surprises us is that many fine people—yes, Christians, if you please—have been caught in one or more of the snares discussed in this book. Many people who have judged others harshly, saying, "I'd never do that," must now ruefully admit that they have. The simple fact is that none of us is immune; given the right circumstances, at the right moment, driven by the right bit of curiosity and euphoria, any one of us could fall into Satan's trap. These snares are as much a warning for me as they are for anyone who would read this book. "So, if you think you are standing firm, be careful that you don't fall!" (1 Corinthians 10:12).

Those of us who have not, for the most part, been caught in these snares have only God and not ourselves to thank. The potential for secret sustained evil exists in all of us. Sometimes, if truth be told, the fear of exposure has kept us from overt sins; or perhaps it was lack of opportunity. More likely, it has been the prayers of parents and friends or the influence of the church that has given us the strength to say no to the temptations that have been carefully hidden along our path. We must be grateful when God intervenes to keep us from those small steps that eventually lead to bigger, more costly ones. As parents we must pray that all of our children's mistakes be small ones.

Say what you will, I believe there are more opportunities to be ensnared by sin today than at any other period of history. First there was television with its powerful seductive images; then came the video revolution, making it possible to show explicit movies in a home with anonymity. Now comes the Internet, with its endless stream of pornography, gambling opportunities, and creative capacity for addictive fascination. These are doorways that sow seeds in the mind that later bear bitter fruit.

I have entitled this book *Seven Snares of the Enemy. Seven,* not because these are the only snares, but because these represent the more popular ways we can be misled. *Snares* because we usually don't set out to become addicts or live with twisted priorities, but situations are presented to us and we are tempted to "take advantage" of them. And, yes, they are usually snares *of the Enemy* laid in our path to trip us in our walk with God. Our temptation is to secretly serve our desires and begin a lifestyle that, if pursued, leads to erosion of character and personal ruin.

This book attempts to accomplish three objectives. First, it should serve as a warning to those who are tempted to explore these avenues of alluring temptation. When we take beginning steps along sinful paths, we may receive much more than we could have bargained for. Jesus taught that when we give ourselves to sin we become its servant; we obey our lusts with focused attention. Blessed are those who have been kept from a lifestyle of secret addictions and pleasures.

Second, in this book I attempt to help us understand why freedom from these sins is so difficult; for example, we will try to enter the mind of an addict so that we can appreciate his struggle and also know how best to help him or her. Many family members and even friends often become enablers, shielding the addict from the very help he needs.

Finally, I try to show that God does have an answer, even for those who have fallen the farthest. As long as someone is alive, we must share a message of hope. Only the truth can set us free. "He who conceals his sins does not prosper, but whoever confesses and renounces them finds mercy" (Proverbs 28:13). Of course, confessing the truth is often costly, but it is a small price to pay for spiritual and moral freedom. We must be brought to a place where we are weary of grieving God; we find freedom when fellowship with Him is more precious to us than our carefully hidden sin.

Is it possible to overcome these "snares" without dependence on God? We all know those who have overcome addictions with therapy, support groups, and sheer willpower. But when God enters the picture, there is a shaking of the foundations and a change in the way we see the world. To those who wish to change their behavior without surrendering their lives to God, I would say that the very core of their lives is built on the wrong premise. There is more to life than the changing of behavior; our deepest need is the change of the heart. The former, we can often do; the latter is God's business. And God's business lies at the heart of the very purpose for living.

Join me as we learn about ourselves and the dangers that lie along our paths. And pray with me that many who read these pages might be introduced to the power of the Son of God, who said, "If the Son sets you free, you will be free indeed" (John 8:36). If there is one primary path for deliverance, it may be simply stated: *We must develop a passion for Christ that is greater than our passion for sin.*

Let's find out if we are willing to follow the truth wherever it might lead.

# WELCOME TO THE WAR

*L*et's be honest, there is a war within.

The heart of a Christian worker was beating wildly as he sat in a Paris hotel room gazing at the street below. He was sorely tempted to leave his room and participate in the sensual pleasures available just a few hundred yards away. Since he was alone, no one would know, and he was quite sure he could control the consequences. Yet he also was troubled by the awareness that God was watching, and perhaps his sin would "find him out." The battle was so intense that, fearing he might succumb, he finally flung his hotel keys onto the street. Only then could he be sure he could never risk leaving his room, for if his keys were not found he could not return there. Better to solve the problem of his lost keys with the hotel staff in the morning than to risk the possibility of ruining his reputation, his marriage, and his ministry.

Most of us ask God to conquer temptation for us by taking away our urge to sin. What we forget is that God wants to give us the ability to say no despite our desires and secret longings. Victory does not come when our choices are made easily, but when we say yes to God when every urge in our body is screaming no. It is not just the weakening of our desires but the strengthening of our resolve that is the path to freedom.

Check this out: There are only two references to the "crown of life" in all the New Testament. In Revelation 2:10 we read that this "crown of life" is given to those who are willing to be martyrs, who are faithful "even to the point of death." Incredibly, the identical crown is given to him who overcomes the test of temptation, because "when he has stood the test, he will receive the crown of life that God has promised to those who love him" (James 1:12). Perhaps the same crown is given to both because mastering our desires is just as difficult as giving our lives for the gospel!

Yes, we've all experienced the conflict between our thoughts and our desires; between what we know is right and what we want to do. Intuitively, we know that the war is between us and God, but this battle soon spills over and engulfs our relationship with others. The outcome of this war determines our character and the legacy we will leave to our children and friends. More important, our wins and losses will affect our standing at the judgment seat of Christ.

Wayne Stiles, in an article titled "Things Are Not Always as They Seem," tells how he was lured into purchasing fourteen CDs from a mail order company that promised he could buy four more at "regular club prices" over a year. Turns out that the price was much higher than he thought, and he soon realized that "the quick benefit so enthralled me that I didn't consider the real price tag."[1]

That is our problem. We are so enticed by quick pleasures that we either forget or simply don't take the time to calculate the price tags. There seem to be so many immediate benefits in taking the path of least resistance that we often give up and follow our desires wherever they lead. Meanwhile, the meter is running, and the price of our negligence zooms off the charts.

"I know chastity is right," the young man said, "but is it smart?" Yes, God may say that immorality is wrong, but even so, a man may seem to be cheating himself out of euphoric pleasure for no really important reason. "Tell me the worst that could happen if I go ahead with an affair," a man trapped in an unhappy marriage asked me. As long as the price wasn't too high, he would disregard God's warning. He would take his chances. "I'll sin today and deal with the devil tomorrow" is a popular philosophy.

Where do we turn when the full effects of our sin begin to reach us? Where do we turn when dabbling turns out to be an addiction, when we find ourselves entangled by our own habits and secret vices? Where do we turn when we begin to realize that sin is not keeping its promise to give us fulfillment?

## THE BATTLE WITHIN

Time was when people had to go looking for stimuli that would fulfill their sensual desires; today, the temptations seek us out, they pursue us. Just surf your television channels and you'll agree that every snare in this book is made attractive in dozens of programs and an endless parade of advertisements. The World Wide Web has much good and helpful information, but it also caters to every perverted passion. Choose your vice, and you can find ways to inflame it, express it, and become addicted to it.

With characteristic insight, the New Testament writer James pinpointed the crux of our battle, saying that we should not blame God when we are tempted. "But each one is tempted, when, by his own evil desire, he is dragged away and enticed. Then, after desire has conceived, it gives birth to sin; and sin, when it is full-grown, gives birth to death" (James 1:14–15). We think sin is a single act, but God sees it as a process.

*Dragged away and enticed!* The phrase "dragged away" has the idea of being caught in a trap and carried away by our captor, and the word "enticed" in the original Greek means "to bait a hook." Both the hunter and the fisherman use bait to capture their unwary prey. No animal would deliberately step into a trap or snap at a hook if it understood the nature of traps and hooks. The hunter promises the prey what it would like to have but in the end gives the prey what he wants it to have! To put it briefly, traps promise one thing but give another. James is telling us that the bait that attracts us conceals deadly poison. If only we believed God's warnings!

Satan himself is abhorrent to us. Knowing that, he comes using different disguises and different names. Just as we use a trap to catch a mouse so we can remain hidden, Satan knows that he too must stay out of sight. Whatever his lure, he is a highly intelligent being who plots our downfall. His intention is to cause us shame and neutralize our effectiveness for Christ. His goal is to get us to do something he wants us to do while making us think the idea is wholly ours. *Behind the lie is the liar; behind the trap is the trapper.*

Satan stalks us without, but our battle begins within. James does not grow weary of pointing out the inner nature of our conflict.

> *What causes fights and quarrels among you?*
> *Don't they come from your desires that battle within you?*
> *You want something but don't get it.*
> *You kill and covet, but you cannot have what you want.*
> *You quarrel and fight.*
> *You do not have, because you do not ask God.*
> *When you ask, you do not receive,*
> *because you ask with wrong motives,*
> *that you may spend what you get on your pleasures.*
>
> —JAMES 4:1–3

James was speaking to Christians who were fighting among themselves. "You kill and covet," he said. They argued over who owned what. Like a subterranean stream, the cauldron was boiling within them, and it spilled out in their relationships. Obviously, they were driven by resentment and the desire to have more. James was not saying that they actually were murdering one another; perhaps he meant that they were guilty of character assassination, destroying the reputation of others. Jesus, you will recall, taught that hating your brother makes you a murderer in your heart. The result was tension and dissension.

James pointed out that strife within individual hearts fueled strife within the church. Like the believers in Corinth, who fractured their membership with allegiance to competing leaders, these people also were dividing, not uniting. Perhaps they quarreled with one another in their daily business. More likely, there were fights within the families, between marriage partners, or between parents and their children. Some people—yes, even Christians—enjoy fighting because they have an ego-need to win.

James said the conflict came from their "desires that battle within you." He meant more than simply their bodily appetites; he wanted his readers to include any hidden fleshly desire that drove them to action. In Greek, the word "desires" is *heedonai,* from which we get the word *hedonism.* These desires are not neutral. He was talking about the desires of the flesh and the gratification of our inward lusts.

Those desires "do battle" within us. The Greek word is a military term that refers to "leading in a battle." That is, our lusts are constantly lining up to array their forces against our spirit, and particularly against the Holy Spirit, who lives within us. The flesh, that is, the lower nature of ours, loves war; it agitates, trying to draw us into a conflict, taking sides with what we know is wrong. These desires fight for a place of prominence; they want to be positioned as in control of the members of our body. The inner sinful nature is determined to win, never accepting defeat. It will "fight to the death."

Paul described the same battle this way: "For I have the desire to do what is good, but I cannot carry it out. For what I do is not the good I want to do; no, the evil I do not want to do—this I keep on doing. . . . So I find this law at work: When I want to do good, evil is right there with me. For in my inner being I delight in God's law; but I see another law at work in the members of my body, waging war against the law of my mind and making me a prisoner of the law of sin at work within my members. What a wretched man I am! Who will rescue me from this body of death? Thanks be to God—through Jesus Christ our Lord!" (Romans 7:18–19, 21–25).

## THE BATTLE DESCRIBED

Let's take a closer look at this war within.

First, these raging desires can take many forms. For some people, it is the urge for revenge. They are motivated by anger, and "getting even" is their way of finding some sort of satisfaction in this unjust world. Or perhaps their anger motivates them to excel for the sake of recognition. For others it could be a feeling of superiority that makes them take advantage of others.

Or look carefully at the alcoholic who tells himself that he is in control of the bottle he holds in his hand. If he were honest he would admit that when he is alone, he really cannot help himself. The bottle seems to cry out, "Curse me a thousand times, and I shall return a thousand and one!" The desire for another drink is stronger than his willpower. It matters not what he knows; it is his desires that rule him.

The man who is a slave to pornography has long since given up the control of his life to the lusts that motivate him. The desires within beg to be satisfied, and pornography promises that euphoric fulfillment is attainable. The same can be said for those who are slaves to greed or those who have a driving urge to dominate the lives of others. In each case, there is a battle over what or who will control the "inner man."

Interestingly, when addicts try to change they often substitute one crutch for another. The alcoholic might turn to prescription drugs to deaden his pain; the recovering gambler might find his refuge in alcohol. Sin has a way of coming in clusters, always surfacing under a different name or under a different disguise. Not until we deal with the root, and not just the fruit, will there be lasting transformation.

We're all fighting a war of some kind, but we should not be mastered by any sin that would want to sit in the driver's seat of our lives. Paul described the conflict: "For the sinful nature desires what is contrary to the Spirit, and the Spirit what is contrary to the sinful nature. They are in conflict with each other, so that you do not do what you want" (Galatians 5:17). Sometimes we surprise ourselves by wanting to do one thing but actually doing another.

Second, these battles are often private; only we know the extent to which we are in conflict with ourselves. We are born sinners and therefore inherit a natural bent toward following our feelings wherever they lead. But down deep we know we are in the wrong, so we hide our shame and guilt from others, and even from ourselves. The conflict within deadens the conscience and leads us ever deeper into the world of isolation and personal defilement.

Third, these desires, if left to themselves, are never satisfied. No matter how often we appease them, they shall return, demanding to be fed one more time. "Death and Destruction are never satisfied, and neither are the eyes of man" (Proverbs 27:20). James put it this way:

"You want something but don't get it" (James 4:2). The meaning is that you set your heart on something, but your fondest dream is not met. Even if you follow your desires, the expected gratification backfires. Your desires promised that, if fulfilled, they would be appeased. You believed them; now they only want more.

Like a man adrift on the ocean, we are convinced that the water around us will slake our thirst. It appears to have all the qualities to do so: it is wet, clear, and accessible. But a single mouthful intensifies our raging thirst. We can never say, "I am now satisfied."

Consider:

- The greedy man meets his objectives but still wants more.
- The gambler will take a bigger risk to recoup his losses.
- The alcoholic swears off the bottle but needs a drink the next day.
- The pornographer will rent another video by the weekend.
- The sex addict, ever searching for complete sexual fulfillment, will seduce another partner soon after he deadens the remorse from his last encounter.
- The pleasure seeker must have more pleasure to deaden the pain caused by seeking pleasure.
- The person dabbling in the occult is propelled ever deeper into spiritual darkness.

Like throwing a piece of meat to a ferocious tiger, the more these appetites are fed, the stronger they return, insisting on more. We promised ourselves that we would always remain in control, but suddenly this promise, like many others, lies broken at our feet. Walter Brueggemann spoke for all of us when he said, "I have found myself discovering that mostly I do not need more advice, but strength. I do not need new information, but the courage, freedom and authorization to act on what I already have been given in the gospel."[2]

Yes, it is usually not a matter of knowledge, for we usually know the difference between right and wrong; it is a matter of desire, a matter of motivation, a matter of *willing* to do what is right. That can only come when we understand the true nature of sin and the path of deliverance. Obviously, we need help from outside of ourselves.

## THE CYCLE OF DEFEAT

Let me give what I call the cycle of defeat.

First, we pride ourselves in being in control. We are confident that we can set the limits of our disobedience. We will allow ourselves a sinful indulgence, but we will be in charge, determining the extent to which we will participate. Just one drink; just one porno movie; just one illicit sexual relationship. *All pleasure and very little risk,* we tell ourselves.

Second, we indulge our desires, but we are also able to win some battles; we find that we can restrain ourselves. We are still convinced that we can stop anywhere along the continuum of disobedience, but we stay in the vicinity of our secret pleasure, just in case we are tempted. And we are.

Third, because the consequences of our disobedience are not immediately evident, we conclude that we have made a reasonable choice. So far, the fulfillment of our secret pleasure seems to outweigh the consequences that we can foresee. The mouse does get to nibble on the cheese, and the fox does enjoy the poisoned meat—for at least a few moments. At this point the trap is still hidden.

Fourth, we sign on the dotted line. Far from satisfying our curiosity, we discover that our awakened desire wants to be fulfilled again. And again. We still convince ourselves that we are in charge. Yes, others have become addicts, but we will not—there are exceptions, just for us. As Mark Twain said, "Of course I'm not addicted to smoking! I've quit a thousand times!"

Fifth, the terms of the agreement are suddenly changed. Just like Gehazi, who thought he was getting gold but ended up with leprosy (2 Kings 5:22–27), we realize that we did not read the fine print. We are not in control anymore; our waking moments are spent thinking about the snare that we have so secretly sought to manage. Now we are forced to live in two worlds, the world of reality and the world of our personal habit.

Sixth, Satan comes to collect. We can't believe what is happening; what was in our control is now out of our hands. We feel a sense of regret and shame that only keeps us bound in our sin. Sometimes our desire for wholeness is much greater than our desire to gratify our lusts, so we try to retrace our steps, seeking freedom from sensual enslavement.

Seventh, in our desperation we cry out to God for a quick deliverance. But He won't bail us out until we've learned our lesson; and at this point, we have not yet learned our lesson, though we think we have. Even yet, we are probably not ready for total repentance.

On and on the cycle goes, until we reach a crisis, a moment of truth, when reality crashes down on us. We are finally desperate enough to do whatever is necessary to be free—no matter the cost.

Of course, I'm not saying that we cannot repent until we have fallen so far that we must reach out to God as our last hope. If our hearts are willing, genuine repentance is possible even if we have not "bottomed out" or otherwise thrown our lives away. We can develop sensitivity toward God and others and enjoy the tough obedience God requires in day-to-day living. Yes, sin need not have the last word.

## OUR BATTLE WITH GOD

Where is God while we struggle?

Give in to our fleshly desires, James says, and God is displeased. "You do not have, because you do not ask God. When you ask, you do not receive, because you ask with wrong motives, that you may spend what you get on your pleasures" (James 4:2–3). When we fall for Satan's lies, our first temptation is to not pray at all but simply to keep going in whatever direction we please. We've all had the experience of wanting something and then realizing that we have not even prayed about it; we have not even given God a chance to give it or withhold it. We just "went for it" because we wanted it. And when we do pray, it is often to fulfill our own pleasures.

I've often asked why so many marriages have turned out so unhappily. I have discovered that many who have walked to the altar have never even asked God about whether this was someone they should marry. Joshua, you will recall, made a foolish decision when he made a treaty with the Gibeonites, because he "did not ask for the counsel of the Lord" (Joshua 9:14 NASB).

Let's reflect on James's words: "When you ask, you do not receive, because you ask with wrong motives, that you may spend what you get on your pleasures." No wonder our prayers aren't answered. We want to squander His blessing on our own "lusts," that is, on our own hedonistic desires. We ask God for wealth, not so that we can feed the hungry, but that we can live a life of luxury; we ask God for health, not so that we might find new ways to please Him, but so we can enjoy our own pleasures. Our prayers are not for others but that we might be content, avoiding the trials of life and participating in the triumphs.

Yes, when we pursue our lusts God is displeased and even becomes our adversary.

> *You adulterous people, don't you know that friendship*
> *with the world is hatred toward God? Anyone who chooses*
> *to be a friend of the world becomes an enemy of God.*
> *Or do you think Scripture says without reason*
> *that the spirit he caused to live in us envies intensely?*
> *But he gives us more grace. That is why the Scripture says:*
> *"God opposes the proud but gives grace to the humble."*
>
> — JAMES 4:4–6

The apostle John defines the world in these terms: "For everything that is in the world—the cravings of sinful man, the lust of his eyes and the boasting of what he has and does—comes not from the Father but from the world. The world and its desires pass away, but the man who does the will of God lives forever" (1 John 2:16–17).

Our love of self, which lies at the heart of our love of the world, breaks the first commandment, "You shall have no other gods before me" (Exodus 20:3). God has given us two hands, but not so that we might hold onto the world with one hand and onto Him with the other. As John says, "Do not love the world or anything in the world. If anyone loves the world, the love of the Father is not in him" (1 John 2:15).

To love the world is to become an adulterer! In the Old Testament, ancient Israel was pictured as being married to Jehovah, "'But like a woman unfaithful to her husband, so you have been unfaithful to me, O house of Israel,' declares the Lord" (Jeremiah 3:20). Psalm 73:27 (KJV) speaks of those who "go a whoring from thee."

Just so in the New Testament, the church is married to Christ. "I am jealous for you with a godly jealousy. I promised you to one husband, to Christ, so that I might present you as a pure virgin to him" (2 Corinthians 11:2). I've counseled women who know the pain of their husband's infidelity. What an insult to their femininity; what a breach of trust, what an arrow that pierces the soul! Of course, many husbands also know the betrayal and grief of a wayward wife.

Let's not miss the point: we betray Christ when we say, in effect, "Though you are my husband, you are not meeting my needs, so I've decided to find another lover." As a pastor who has tried to put marriages together that were torn apart by adultery, I think I can grasp the heartache and disloyalty the Lord feels when we have other lovers in whom we delight.

Yes, the battle within affects us and those who know us, but it affects Christ much more. Imagine the personal affront our worldly adulteries are to him! Thomas Guthrie used to say, "If you find yourself loving any pleasure better than your prayers, any book better than the Bible, any house better than the house of God, any table better than the Lord's table, any persons better than Christ, any indulgence better than the hope of Heaven—*take alarm*" (italics mine).[3]

If we fall in love with the world, not only are we adulterers, but we also hate God. "Don't you know," James asked, "that friendship with the world is hatred toward God?" (James 4:4). Think of how insensitive we are if we think that we can love the world and God at the same time. We forget that God is grieved because of our sin, since it is directed toward Him personally. We might not think that we hate God, but if we love our sin, we despise Him.

James continued, "Or do you think Scripture says without reason that the spirit he caused to live in us envies intensely?" (James 4:5). A probable interpretation is that this speaks of the agony that the Holy Spirit must endure when he sees us turning away from God to give our affection to the world. The Spirit jealously guards our relationship with God; He is grieved when we transfer our affection to the world.

To review: James began by saying that we are at war with others: there are "fights and quarrels among you." Then he said that we are at war with ourselves. We have "desires" that arise within us. All of this leads to being at war with God. Left to ourselves, we are a warring people who strike out in many different directions. We've all known those who are at war with God and therefore at war with themselves.

Serpents are coiled on the bottom of our hearts, vying for an opportunity to spew their poisonous venom throughout the soul. We must be in a constant state of alert, for the enemy within is in cahoots with the Enemy without. "Above all else, guard your heart, for it is the wellspring of life" (Proverbs 4:23).

## OUR BATTLE CAN BE WON

Indwelling sin does not absolve us of responsibility for our actions. Today, we commonly hear that men commit adultery because of their genetic makeup; indeed, it is fashionable to say that love does not exist but is only an innate desire to breed offspring. Since it is "natural" to desire other partners, we are told it is not wrong, just inconvenient.

Homosexuals say they are "born that way," so their behavior must be excused. A kleptomaniac I knew argued that he should not be held responsible for stealing, because he also was "born that way." A television program told the story of identical twins who were adopted by two sets of nondrinking parents. Yet both twins, growing up in separate parts of the country, became alcoholics, following the lead of their natural father. This was said to be proof that some alcoholics are "born that way."

So scientists want to find that alcoholic gene, that gambler gene, that adulterer gene, that kleptomaniac gene, and, yes, that homosexual gene. Suppose these mystery genes are found? What conclusion should we draw from that discovery? Actually, if the researchers had read their Bibles, they would already know that all of us were born with sinful, perverted desires. Left to ourselves, we will turn from God, fulfill our lusts, and choose the sin that gives us the most pleasure. Yes, we are all "born that way."

Sin is genetic. Thanks to the genetic makeup of our parents, sin is passed on to us. So we should not be surprised if there is a homosexual gene, an alcoholic gene, an adultery gene, a thievery gene; we most assuredly all have a rebellious gene, a self-righteous gene. We all have a severe genetic problem that makes us what we are. Yes, sinful tendencies are passed on from parents to the child.

Our hope for change is based on the fact that our human spirit (that part of us that thinks, wills, and chooses) is influenced by our genes but not controlled by them. At least we have the power to make some choices, no matter how much we feel driven by our sinful impulses. For example, we can choose to cry to God for help; we can choose to enlist the help of others in our struggle against sin. We are not locked into any sinful addiction or lifestyle unless we believe we are.

When we play the "blame game" and fail to take personal responsibility, we rationalize, telling ourselves that change is impossible. We must be so humbled before God that we are willing to take responsibility for our sinful desires, though they might appear involuntary. Regardless of our condition, we must agree with David, "Against you, you only, have I sinned and done what is evil in your sight" (Psalm 51:4).

We attract the attention of God when we are finally willing to give up our excuses, when all of our rationalizations fall by the wayside in the light of His holiness. Certainly, we cannot do what we ought; but the message of salvation is that Christ did for us what we cannot: He met God's requirements for those who believe on Him. And He stands by to help those who are most helpless and know it.

Satan has two lies he wants us to believe. The first is "Just try my way once and you will be satisfied . . . *once* will not matter." So we fall into one of his snares and find ourselves trapped, and just possibly our lives might be spiraling out of control. Then he comes along with a second lie: "Now that you have fallen, there is no use standing up again . . . *you are mine.*" Both are lies; both have to be confronted and broken.

James has a word for us.

*Submit yourselves, then, to God. Resist the devil, and he will flee*
*from you. Come near to God and he will come near to you.*
*Wash your hands, you sinners, and purify your hearts,*
*you double-minded. Grieve, mourn and wail.*

*Change your laughter to mourning and your joy to gloom.*
*Humble yourselves before the Lord, and he will lift you up.*

—JAMES 4:7–10

*Submit to God.* How will that free me from my conflict? Does this mean that I will no longer face temptation? Will my love of sensuality disappear? Will the urge to drink or gamble vanish? Will everyone, from now on, treat me just right?

No, submission means that I give God my rights. I give Him the right to intervention. I am finally willing to do anything and everything to be free of the sin that entangles me. In effect, we say, "I give up all excuses; I will, with God's help, burn all the bridges that lead me back to my old lifestyle. The prospect of having a clean conscience and living in fellowship with God is more attractive than the pleasures whose empty promises I have believed. At last I lay down the weapons of a rebel. I make a commitment to a life of holiness, whatever the cost."

*Resist the devil.* What does the devil have to do with it? He takes the sins in which I delight and strengthens their grip. He makes sin look good to us; he is the one who puts up a sign that says, "This way to happiness." What is more, he inserts ideas into our minds that we think are our own. In fact, it is he who desires to entrap us, to appeal to our weakness and destroy us. "Be self-controlled and alert. Your enemy the devil prowls around like a roaring lion looking for someone to devour. Resist him, standing firm in the faith, because you know that your brothers throughout the world are undergoing the same kind of sufferings" (1 Peter 5:8–9).

*Wash your hands, you sinners, and purify your hearts, you double-minded.* James is saying that we should be cleansed from sin, receiving God's forgiveness for our waywardness. When we confess our sins, it must be with the intention that God would not only forgive us but rid us of their power. If we have a casual attitude toward sin, we will never triumph over it.

*Humble yourselves before the Lord.* Yes, it is true that God humbles us; but we can humble ourselves. Humility is a choice I make in the presence of God. Pride keeps me from sharing my need with others; pride keeps me bound in the secrecy of my sins and failures. Pride says that I must look good, no matter what. Pride says that even if I stumble, no one can know about my failures. The promise is that if we humble ourselves, the Lord will "lift us up."

James believed we could be different.

There is that old story of an Indian who described his war within his heart as two dogs fighting each other. "There is a dark, angry dog who fights from the shadows; then there is a good dog who fights in the light."

"Which one wins?" he was asked.

"The one I feed the most."

## HOW TO USE THIS BOOK

There are some sins that are particularly stubborn; the behavioral ruts run so deep that changing lifestyles is difficult, some would say impossible. Our sinful natures by themselves are powerful enough to cause the conflicts we've described. But add to this the outer stimuli available today, and the chains of habit can become tighter and more formidable.

We've already introduced the word "addiction," which is best defined as preoccupation with the "blinding absorption of sin." Today we are familiar with groups such as Alcoholics Anonymous, Gambler's Anonymous, and the like. All these groups are an acknowledgment of special habits that need special treatment. However, some people simply will not attend a support group, fearing the shame and embarrassment that comes with the admission that one's life is "out of control."

I pray first that this book will be a point of entrance into the lives of many, especially when they realize that their particular "snare" is shared by millions of others. "No temptation has seized you except what is common to man. And God is faithful; he will not let you be tempted beyond what you can bear. But when you are tempted, he will also provide a way out so that you can stand up under it" (1 Corinthians 10:13). When we know that we are not alone in our struggles; when we discover the roots of our addictions and realize that we are all fighting some battle, we are more ready to admit, "I need help."

I also hope that many will be led to help family members and friends who struggle with addictions but are too ashamed to seek help and counsel. In other words, this is not just a handbook on spiritual warfare, but hopefully also gives insights to counselors and family members who are acquainted with those who are hurting but do not know where to turn. Never give up hope, for as a friend of mine says, *a tendency is not necessarily a destiny.*

Second, this book was written to help us understand those who have fallen into one snare or another. Condemnation is easy, but understanding is more difficult. Why doesn't the pornographer just quit his habit? Why doesn't the alcoholic just say no to his bottle once for all? Why does the sex offender not just stop searching for partners? In this book I try, as best I can, to "get into the mind" of the addict to show why it is often impossible to reason with him; not until we know how an addict views the world are we ready to give him help.

Finally, this book can be used as a primer for personal deliverance. This does not mean that the path to spiritual freedom is easy; indeed, some who read this book are in for the fight of their lives. I am heartened by the words of the angel to Joseph, "She will give birth to a son, and you are to give him the name Jesus, because *he will save his people from their sins*" (Matthew 1:21, italics added).

Let me say once more that this book is a warning to those who have not yet fallen into the snares that our Enemy has laid out for us. It is always easier to defend territory in one's possession than it is to reclaim ground that has been lost. How much better never to have taken a drink than to fight alcoholism; how much better never to have gambled than to fight the urge to "strike it rich." Yes, those who have been preserved from the more outward expression of these sins are most fortunate. I pray that this book will increase their gratitude to God for past victories and warn them of the high cost of these hidden sins.

If Jesus can only forgive and not deliver His people from their sins, then He is not the Savior the New Testament presents Him to be. Listen to His words: "The thief comes only to steal and kill and destroy; I have come that they may have life, and have it to the full" (John 10:10). *Life to the full!* That surely must include freedom from the snares that have deceived us.

Finally, it is preferable, though not necessary, to read the chapters in this book in sequence. Each chapter does stand alone in describing a particular "snare" and then giving direction on the path to spiritual freedom. However, only if you read the entire book will you find a more comprehensive understanding of the nature of our struggle with sin and God's prescription for our need.

Join me as we learn together.

## A PRAYER TO BEGIN THE JOURNEY

*Father, I pray that You will give me the desire to change. Long ago I concluded that I cannot help myself in the struggle against sin. Show me that things can be different; grant me the grace to follow through with any commitments I make.*

*At this time I affirm that I belong to You, and as best as I know how, I surrender myself to You; more than that, I look to the risen Christ, confident that everything You ask me to do is based on what He has already done. Help me not to fear, but to proceed in hope and faith.*

*I come under Your authority that I might exercise Your authority as a member of Your family. I resist Satan that he might flee from me. Help me to be willing to "resist unto death" against the sins that entangle me.*

*In Jesus' name, Amen.*

# GREED:
# THE HEART
# REVEALED

$T$he point is, ladies and gentleman, that greed, for lack of a better word, is good. Greed is right. Greed works. Greed clarifies, cuts through and captures the essence of the evolutionary spirit. Greed in all of its forms—greed for life, money, love and knowledge—has marked the upward surge of mankind." So said Michael Douglas in a movie video clip that I saw recently.[1]

Contrast his words with that of another:

> *"No servant can serve two masters. Either he will hate the one and love the other, or he will be devoted to the one and despise the other. You cannot serve both God and Money."*
> *The Pharisees, who loved money, heard all this and were sneering at Jesus. He said to them, "You are the ones who justify yourselves in the eyes of men, but God knows your hearts. What is highly valued among men is detestable in God's sight."*
>
> —LUKE 16:13–15

Money, *detestable in the sight of God!*

Whom shall we believe, Christ or Michael Douglas? Christ or Ivan F. Boeske?

*Who wants to be a millionaire?* Turns out that one of TV's most popular shows has uncovered many people who want to get rich quick. Down deep in our hearts, all of us would like to be millionaires. The lure of big money has the power to make even decent people compromise their principles. On this rock many a life has been dashed to pieces.

Greed has many different forms. Greed is not just the sin of Wall Street; the sin of the obsessed day trader, spending every waking minute peering into his computer monitor. Greed is not just the sin of the wealthy but of those who would live beyond their means, those who make unwise choices, mortgaging their future for the present.

Take, for example, a couple whom we will call Paul and Julie, who were married in their early twenties. They lived in an apartment for two years but, in order to establish equity, bought a house with a down payment borrowed from Paul's father. They also bought some new furniture, enticed by the lure that they would not have to make payments until next year.

Their relocation meant that they needed a second car, and they decided to get a relatively new one, based on a promise that Paul would receive an increase in salary. But when Julie's job was terminated, they found it difficult to make all the payments. One day they flipped on a light switch and discovered that their electricity had been cut off.

To shield his wife from financial pressures, Paul didn't tell her about some other loans he had made to finance his growing burden of debt. In order to meet their financial shortfall, Paul took a second loan on the house and a temporary loan from his father-in-law. Although Julie found a part-time job, they simply could not keep up with the pressure of the regular bills. Paul was angry with Julie when she put $40.00 on the offering plate one Sunday, because they could not afford it. In fact, they were beginning to put their groceries on credit cards. Paul even began gambling on the side, hoping for "the big win."

When Julie discovered she was pregnant, the arguments escalated. Julie suspected that her husband was being dishonest with her;

he kept trying to tell her that eventually they would pull out of their debt. He just needed her to be patient. But when he later suggested they file bankruptcy, Julie was stunned. Because she felt he had so badly handled their finances and was dishonest, Julie was contemplating a divorce.

Where did they go wrong? Yes, believe it or not, greed, like a weed, found a home in their hearts. Though "the love of things" seemed both harmless and acceptable by today's standards, this tiny plant began to exert greater control over this couple's lives. In the end, greed led them to take a series of missteps.

First, they borrowed money rather than be satisfied with God's provision. Before credit cards were popular, Christians would trust God for a car, for furniture, or for a home. God, it was believed, would lead his people by supplying money or withholding it; if He wanted them to have a refrigerator, He would supply money for it, and if not, a friend would choose to donate a secondhand model. At any rate, back then the words "Give us this day our daily bread" had real meaning.

Today, faith is out and credit is in. I see nothing wrong with borrowing for items that appreciate in value; but it is counterproductive to borrow for items that diminish in value. My wife and I have taken out some wise loans and some unwise ones. We've learned that we should only use a credit card for convenience, not to accumulate things for which we do not have the money. Only about 6 percent of card users pay them off every month. If you can't control yourself, then fulfill your childhood dream and play doctor: take your credit cards and perform plastic surgery!

The seed of greed is planted when we are discontent with what we have. "In the desert the whole community grumbled against Moses and Aaron. The Israelites said to them, 'If only we had died by the LORD's hand in Egypt! There we sat around pots of meat and ate all the food we wanted, but you have brought us out into this desert to starve this entire assembly to death" (Exodus 16:2–3). God chose to give them manna, promising that it would form on the ground every morning but be stale the next day.

God was not amused with their grumbling, but took it as a personal insult. Moses said, "You will know that it was the Lord when he gives you meat to eat in the evening and all the bread you want in the morning, because he has heard your grumbling against him. Who are we? You are not grumbling against us, but against the LORD" (v. 8). Obviously, if they had been thankful for what they did have, God would have continued to provide, perhaps even giving something better than manna.

In another version of what happened, God is pictured as very angry over Israel's complaint that they were not getting the meat they wanted. Moses, speaking for God, said, "Now the LORD will give you meat, and you will eat it. You will not eat it for just one day, or two days, or five, ten or twenty days, but for a whole month—until it comes out of your nostrils and you loathe it—because you have rejected the LORD, who is among you, and have wailed before him, saying, 'Why did we ever leave Egypt?'" (Numbers 11:18–20). Discontentment lies at the heart of our struggle with greed.

God may withhold money for a reason. We need to give Him time to meet our need, being willing to wait for His provision. Yes, though purchasing items on credit is popular today, and most of us have done it, borrowing has the inherent danger of fostering distrust of God; it takes responsibilities He has promised to carry and puts them on our shoulders. We might be quite convinced that our motivation is not greed, just meeting the needs of daily life. But discontentment is the seed that eventually leads us to want more and more, if only we had the opportunity.

Second, the story of Paul and Julie illustrates how the one small sin of greed can lead to a second sin of dishonesty. Thus, a marriage that began with so much happiness ended in failure when Paul concealed information from his wife and manipulated accounts. Greed, as we shall see, never travels alone. It is always accompanied by other sins.

Finally, Tim and Julie put themselves in a predicament where they were unable to give money to the Lord's work. Every dime was needed to keep the creditors away from the door. Feeling the pressure to meet the minimum payment on their credit card, they had to stop their giving to the church and missions. Julie, bless her, wanted to give, but when Paul objected, they backed off.

## IDENTIFYING GREED

Greed comes in many different forms. Some men refuse to give their wives money, not for lack but for stinginess. They will pinch every penny and moan over every expenditure. For them, money is so closely identified with who they are that the thought of parting with it is almost unbearable. Some find it difficult to write the checks for their utilities and groceries.

How shall we describe greed?

Greed lies at the heart of consumerism and is often a mask for painful feelings of emptiness and a tendency to respond to the advertising that bombards us from every angle. At its worst, it is a self-centered narcissism empowered by affluence, a lack of meaning, and a resistance to God. "Huge shopping malls have become the cathedrals of our society for millions of worshiping shopaholics."[2] As the bumper sticker puts it, "When the going gets tough, the tough go shopping." Easy credit makes it possible for even the poor to "shop till you drop."

Greed has two cousins. The first is covetousness, the desire to have what others possess. We see the elegant home that a friend has purchased, and in our hearts we want to own the same or better. We hear that a relative has made a million dollars in the stock market, and we wish we had his bank account. These kinds of thoughts are so much a part of who we are that we do not see them as sinful but just a part of the normal course of life. How differently God sees it all!

The second sin that accompanies greed is envy. If covetousness means that I want what others have, envy means that I resent the blessings others have received. "Envy is discontent or ill will at another's good fortune, because one wishes it would have been his; dislike for a person who has what one wants."[3] The poor often envy the rich. The weak envy the strong. Those of ordinary physical attributes are tempted to envy the attractive; the overlooked are tempted to envy those who receive all the attention. Envy will cause a mother to murder a girl who bested her daughter in a beauty contest.

There is a story in Jewish folklore about a store owner who was visited by an angel. The angel offered the man a wish that would give him anything he desired. However, there was one condition—his rival, whom he envied intensely, would receive double of the wish granted. Without hesitation, the envious man wished to be blind in one eye. Cain's envy of Abel led to murder. Saul tried to kill David because the lad made the king look bad. Envy caused the fall of Satan; it is the sin that put Jesus on the cross.

In one of the saddest stories in the Bible, a young man lost his eternal soul because of greed. When he met Jesus, he asked: "Teacher, what good thing must I do to get eternal life?" (Matthew 19:16). When Jesus told him that he should keep the commandments, he quite honestly replied that he had—at least he thought so. Jesus, knowing the man's heart better than he himself did, said, "If you want to be perfect, go, sell your possessions and give to the poor, and you will have treasure in heaven. Then come, follow me" (v. 21). The young man had received an answer he neither expected nor liked; forced to make a decision, he walked away. "When the young man heard this, he went away sad, because he had great wealth" (v. 22).

Obviously, Jesus was not teaching that we get to heaven by our own good deeds; generosity will not save us. But He wanted this young man to see how covetous his heart really was. As far as we know, he never returned to follow Jesus. Parting with his money was more painful than the prospect of losing the eternal life he knew he wanted. Like the man who drowned because he loaded his pockets with gold when the ship was sinking, this young man's money caused him to lose sight of the Lord who could save him.

Life has few certainties, but this is one of them:

> *For of this you can be sure: No immoral, impure or*
> *greedy person—such a man is an idolater—has any inheritance*
> *in the kingdom of Christ and of God. Let no one deceive you*
> *with empty words, for because of such things*
> *God's wrath comes on those who are disobedient.*
> *Therefore do not be partners with them.*
>
> —EPHESIANS 5:5–7

Notice that the first commandment, "You shall have no other gods before me," and the last commandment, "You shall not covet," are actually the same commandment (Exodus 20:3, 17). Greed, said Paul, is idolatry. Covetousness is active rivalry against God. Eve coveted being like God and took the forbidden fruit. Lot's wife coveted Sodom and was turned into a pillar of salt. David coveted his neighbor's wife and received heartache for himself and a broken family.

How powerful is the lure of easy money? Years ago the New Era scheme promised investors that their money would double every ten or eleven months. Some organizations profited, and this was seen as evidence that the plan was working. Many red flags were ignored by investors who insisted that the "proof was in the pudding." Some people refused to ask the hard questions, wanting so desperately to get in on the financial windfall.

The *Wall Street Journal* says that these questions caused some auditors and board members of organizations to suggest caution, "but these voices were drowned out by those that pointed to the indisputable: New Era had never failed to double participants' money." The article goes on to say that nobody stopped to sniff the air. One man who discouraged his college from participating in New Era's program, but without success, said, "They could just taste the money. . . . The weakness around the mouth, the desire in the eyes. I've always heard the expression, 'You can see greed written,' but I've seen the reality."[4]

Greed crouches like a beast within our hearts and is so much a part of us that we cannot see it objectively. Dangle big money in someone's face and he or she just might throw aside the most dearly held principles to get it. Even Christian relatives will fight over a will, stepping on anyone or anything that stands in their way. "A greedy man brings trouble to his family, but he who hates bribes will live" (Proverbs 15:27).

Isaiah leveled God's judgment toward the spiritual leadership of his day. "Israel's watchmen are blind, they all lack knowledge; they are all mute dogs, they cannot bark; they lie around and dream, they love to sleep. They are dogs with mighty appetites; they never have enough. They are shepherds who lack understanding; they all turn to their own way, each seeks his own gain" (Isaiah 56:10–11). *Mighty appetites, but never enough.*

## A STORY OF GREED

One day Jesus was interrupted to settle a family quarrel. As all rabbis, He was often asked questions about the application of the law to daily life. Apparently in this instance an elder brother refused to give his younger brother the one-third of the inheritance that was his by law. "Teacher, tell my brother to divide the inheritance with me" (Luke 12:13). Perhaps it was this man's only opportunity to ask Jesus a question, and he used the opportunity to put pressure on his family to be fair about the inheritance.

Squabbling among relatives after the death of a family member is, of course, nothing new. A funeral director in Chicago told me that on one occasion family members drew guns in the cemetery after the death of a wealthy man. Of course, nice families don't do it that way; they politely wait to have their arguments later and then refuse to talk to one another for the rest of their lives.

Jesus could have solved this problem by urging a settlement of the dispute. But rather than treat this as a legal problem, He broke the outer shell and revealed the covetousness of the human heart. The law can force people to make outward changes, but only God can change the motivation. "Watch out! Be on your guard against all kinds of greed; a man's life does not consist in the abundance of his possessions," Jesus warned (Luke 12:15).

To make his point, Jesus told a story about a rich man:

*"The ground of a certain rich man*
*produced a good crop. He thought to himself,*
*'What shall I do? I have no place to store my crops.'*
*"Then he said, 'This is what I'll do. I will tear down my barns*
*and build bigger ones, and there I will store all my grain and my*
*goods. And I'll say to myself, "You have plenty of good things laid*
*up for many years. Take life easy; eat, drink and be merry."'*
*"But God said to him, 'You fool! This very night*
*your life will be demanded from you. Then who will*
*get what you have prepared for yourself?'*
*"This is how it will be with anyone who stores up*
*things for himself but is not rich toward God."*
—LUKE 12:16–21

What mistakes did this greedy man make?

## He Mistook His Body for His Soul

When he was speaking to himself, he used the Greek word *psyche,* which means soul. "And I will say to my soul, 'Soul, you have many goods laid up for many years to come; take your ease, eat, drink and be merry" (Luke 12:19 NASB). He should have said, "I will say to my *body,* you have many goods laid up for years to come." Wealth had become his center of gravity. His body was full, but his soul was starved.

He might have stood as a wonderful physical specimen, but spiritually he was disconnected; he had not learned that "a man's life does not consist in the abundance of his possessions" (Luke 12:15). He was placing ultimate value on something that was of passing worth. He was selling his soul for bargain-basement prices.

Come with me to Wall Street, or LaSalle Street. Come with me to the banks and stock exchanges of the world. Come where investors are shouting, where the markets are rising, and where money is being made. Come and ask those who are driven by greed—ask them about their souls. You'll discover that there is no room for serious God-talk at the end of a good trading day. The delights of the body, *yes;* the filling of the soul, *no.*

Come with me to the health clubs, where people spend an hour or more each day, trying to get in shape, sculpturing their bodies and applying the latest oils and artificial tans. Then let us stop at the health food store, where people buy the right vegetables and vitamins to eke out a few more months' existence. Ask these people if they are as serious about the forgiveness of their sins as they are the toxins in potatoes.

There is an old legend that Midas, one of the Phrygian kings, was told by the gods that any wish he made would be fulfilled. He requested that whatever he touched would turn to gold. At first he felt fortunate, but when the very food he touched changed to gold, he begged the gods to rescind his "blessing." Jesus asked, "What good is it for a man to gain the whole world, yet forfeit his soul?" (Mark 8:36).

Yes, the body is important, but Jesus taught that the soul is more important still. Hear it from His own lips. "Do not be afraid of those who kill the body but cannot kill the soul. Rather, be afraid of the One who can destroy both soul and body in hell" (Matthew 10:28). The body will perish, but the soul endures.

## He Mistook Himself for God

Six times this rich man used the pronoun "I," and if you add the number of times he used other personal pronouns, the total is eleven or twelve. Let's read it the way he might have said it. "He thought to *himself*, 'What shall *I* do? *I* have no place to store *my* crops.' Then he said, 'This is what *I* will do. *I* will tear down *my* barns and build bigger ones, and there *I* will store all *my* grain and goods. And *I'll* say to *myself*, '*You* have plenty of good things laid up for many years. Take life easy; eat, drink, and be merry.'"

He forgot that he was only a steward, a man who was put on this earth to dispense the wealth of Another. He forgot that God is the only owner and we are accountable for the way we manage His gifts. In a word, he took God's place.

What did he mean by "*my* crops"? Did he create the kernels of grain and program them to grow and reproduce? Did he create the soil with the right balance of nutrients so that the plants would grow to their best ability? Did he create the sun that would shine with just the right intensity? And what about the rain?

And what about *my* retirement fund? *My* stocks? *My* mutual funds? *My* bank account? *My* home? *My* car?

When our dependence shifts from God to riches, we have put ourselves and our possessions in the place of God. Riches are deceitful for the simple reason that they give us a false sense of security. There is a story about a prospector caught in the gold rush. He had stayed too long in the riverbed and was caught in the snow. When he was found dead in his hut, a bag of gold was lying next to him, but it could not feed him. His money could not bring him warmth; it could not restore his depleted body back to health.

## He Mistook Time for Eternity

This man lived as though this was the only world that mattered. He acted as if his future was in his hands. "You have plenty of good things laid up for many years," he mused. How could he be so sure? He thought his future was in his hands, but that very night he learned that no matter how tightly we grasp our wealth, it never leaves God's hands and His sovereign control.

That night his soul was *demanded* of him. This word in Greek was used when a person had borrowed money and now the note was due. God had given this man wealth and riches; God had given him crops he did not deserve. And now the day of accounting had arrived.

At his funeral, people no doubt spoke highly of his skill as a farmer and of his good fortune. But he, along with another rich fool, was in hades, being tormented. Beautiful words spoken about him, had he heard them, would have only added to his remorse and shame. A minute after he died, he knew that he was hemmed in and his future no longer under his control. He had an overwhelming realization that his eternity was irrevocably fixed, and his future would only become worse, not better.

## GOD'S JUDGMENT ON GREED

The book of Revelation has an incredible description of the coming collapse of all financial empires at a time when all the souls on planet Earth will be demanded by God.

Symbolized as the city of Babylon, the collapse of this giant metropolis will cause wonder and astonishment.

*"When the kings of the earth who committed adultery with her*
*and shared her luxury see the smoke of her burning,*
*they will weep and mourn over her. Terrified at her torment,*
*they will stand far off and cry:*

*"'Woe! Woe, O great city,*
*O Babylon, city of power!*
*In one hour your doom has come!'*

*"The merchants of the earth will weep and mourn over her be-*
*cause no one buys their cargoes any more—cargoes of gold, silver,*
*precious stones and pearls; fine linen, purple, silk and scarlet*
*cloth; every sort of citron wool, and articles of every kind made of*
*ivory, costly wood, bronze, iron and marble; cargoes of cinnamon*
*and spice, of incense, myrrh and frankincense, of wine and olive*
*oil, of fine flour and wheat; cattle and sheep;*
*horses and carriages; and bodies and souls of men. . . .*

*"'Woe! Woe, O great city,*
*dressed in fine linen, purple and scarlet,*
*and glittering with gold, precious stones and pearls!*
*In one hour such great wealth has been brought to ruin!'"*

—REVELATION 18:11–13, 16–17

Somewhere I read a story about a girl who herded cattle, thinking that holding a coin for a day was her reward. We too are given a
coin for a day, and in the end we will give an account to God for it.
In that sense, life is like the game of Monopoly, where we are all hand-
ed our cards, but in the end everything goes back into the box. Only
that which is done for God has eternal rewards. David Livingstone
said, "I will place no value on anything I have except its relationship
to Jesus Christ and His kingdom."

Years ago I saw a movie in which the east end of a house was in
flames, but the family at the west end continued their renovation as if
they would live there for the next ten years. One was painting, another gluing wallpaper, and a third was scrubbing the shelves. The Bible
assures us that someday "the heavens will disappear with a roar . . . and
the earth and everything in it will be laid bare." Then follows a question. "Since everything will be destroyed in this way, what kind of people ought you to be? You ought to live holy and godly lives as you
look forward to the day of God and speed its coming" (2 Peter 3:10–12).

## UPROOTING THE SIN OF GREED

How can we put the ax to the root of this tree? Greed exists under layers of denial, conditioning, and rationalizations. This is one of

40

those instances where we simply "don't get it." The love of money is so much a part of who we are that we can't see it unless we take the time to meditate, think, and pray. If we look carefully, it will be found lurking within our money-loving hearts.

In the parable of the sower, Jesus identified different kinds of soils upon which the seed falls. He said, "Still others, like seed sown among thorns, hear the word; but the worries of this life, the *deceitfulness of wealth* and the desires for other things come in and choke the word, making it unfruitful" (Mark 4:18–19, italics added). The reason wealth is deceitful is that though we need money to live, it quickly grasps for our affections.

First, we must admit that greed exists in our hearts. Greed is difficult to detect because society has no stigma against it. Like a fish that cannot see the water, so we cannot see the monster that lurks within us. Only God can help us by both showing us our sin and giving us the motivation and power to overcome it. We love to hear stories of misers who die in a hovel without adequate food and after their death relatives discover thousands of dollars. We say, "Now there is a person who is greedy." We have a warm, comfy feeling when we hear a story like that because we know that that is not us. In comparison, we are very generous. So we define greed out of existence.

When a multimillionaire tycoon on Wall Street is caught in insider trading, hoping to make more millions, we say, "That is greed." We refuse to acknowledge that our own pittance we put in the offering plate each Sunday is a sign of greed; we refuse to admit that our own hoarding is greed. We refuse to admit that greed is paying more attention to the stock market than we do to the Bible.

Or we define greed as prudence. We justify our stinginess by reminding ourselves that only the *love* of money is the root of all evil. Then we tell ourselves that we really don't *love* it; we might romance it, ruminate on it, worry that we might lose it, but we really don't *love* it.

We might not think of greed when we are unfair with our employees; we might not think of greed when we spend more time thinking about the stock market than we do the Bible. We don't think of greed when we give miserly to the cause of missions and the work of our church. Our problem is that we don't see greed for the monster it is, that evil monster who refuses to die in our hearts.

Second, we must ask: To what extent are we content with God? Greed can take the place of God so easily for the simple reason that it makes the same promises God does. Money says, "If you get enough of me, I promise I will never leave you or forsake you. I will be with you when the stock market is up; I will be with you when it is down. I will be there for you when you are sick and be there for you when you are old."

Think of the promises wealth made to the rich fool. "You have plenty of good things laid up for many years. Take life easy; eat, drink and be merry" (Luke 12:19). Wealth promised to give this man the good life, but that was exactly the promise Jesus made to His followers: "I have come that [you] might have life, and have it to the full" (John 10:10). God knows that greed is a serious contender for our affections.

Love of money and love of God are mutually exclusive. Speaking of the competition, Jesus said, "No one can serve two masters. Either he will hate the one and love the other, or he will be devoted to the one and despise the other. You cannot serve both God and Money" (Matthew 6:24). God hates greed because He knows that when money meets our needs we rely on the money rather than on Him. That's why covetousness is, figuratively speaking, a slap in God's face.

Paul understood this.

*Command those who are rich in this present world*
*not to be arrogant nor to put their hope in wealth,*
*which is so uncertain, but to put their hope in God,*
*who richly provides us with everything for our enjoyment.*
*Command them to do good, to be rich in good deeds,*
*and to be generous and willing to share.*
*In this way they will lay up treasure for themselves*
*as a firm foundation for the coming age,*
*so that they may take hold of the life that is truly life.*

—1 TIMOTHY 6:17–19

It comes to this: Will God meet our needs, or will He not? Does God satisfy those who depend on Him, or do we need more money in order to be happy? Paul says that "godliness with contentment is great gain" (1 Timothy 6:6). Thus it must be either greed or God.

Third, the hard part is to genuinely surrender all we have to God. I've found that the more honest we are in our commitment, the more difficult this submission becomes. To lay everything before the Lord—every bank account, mutual fund, house, and car—to give the control over these to God requires an act of faith we are prone to resist. Not until there is this death to self can we begin to slay the monster of covetousness. Here at last the battle lines are clear: God will have no rivals.

In the beginning, the issues were clear: God owned everything, and Adam and Eve were simply managers of His property. But the Fall made them thieves, desiring to own that which belonged to Another. Ever since, God has had to wrest the goddess of greed from our hearts, to bring us back to the reality that we cannot call anything our own. As managers we must admit to theft and return our stolen goods back to our Master.

Fourth, we must "give our greed away." When we give our money, we give ourselves, and in so doing we give away our stingy heart. Many of us could double the amount we give to the Lord's work and still live comfortably. That would be a wonderful step in sapping the strength out of the "monster of more." Giving is not an overflow valve that you open when your coffers overflow; it is the natural, daily flow of a life that has learned to depend on God.

Not a one of us can overcome this sin that God hates unless we are generous in our giving. When Paul wanted to motivate believers toward generosity, he used Christ as an example. "For you know the grace of our Lord Jesus Christ, that though he was rich, yet for your sakes he became poor, so that you through his poverty might become rich" (2 Corinthians 8:9). The ultimate antidote to selfishness is the cross. Unless we are willing to take our place with Christ there, we will always live for ourselves and not for God.

A missionary couple I know decided to put God to the test in the matter of money. They agreed to never go into debt but to trust God for their funds. They would buy nothing unless they could pay for it in cash; in this way they could determine the Lord's leading for many of their decisions. What is more, the greater their need, the more they gave. Now, thirty years later, they can affirm that God has been faithful. They not only have had their needs met with many blessings along the way, but they proved that the more we give to God's work the more He rewards us with blessings and help.

Michael Douglas was wrong. Greed is not good. Greed does not "work" within the kingdom. In fact, greed stands in direct opposition to God and lies at the heart of all other sins. *Lord, deliver us!*

## A PRAYER TO BEGIN THE JOURNEY

*Father, according to Your Word, You have "searched me and known me." I confess that covetousness is idolatry. Now, Lord, show me what You see. Help me to be obedient to what You reveal to me. In faith I surrender all of my assets to You: my mutual funds, my bank accounts, and all of my holdings. I take this prayer as a transfer of ownership, realizing that it already was in Your hands. I give You my ability to earn money and pray that You will guide me in my giving to Your work. As You lead me down the pathway of generosity, make me a willing travel companion. Let this prayer be the first of many affirming the decision that I make today. Let me always respond to new information You bring to my attention.*

*In Jesus' name, Amen.*

# GAMBLING: IS IT A GOOD BET?

*I*f you had known Jeff, you would never have believed he would end up in jail. But in high school he began to wager on sports and play the slot machines. When he put a huge wager on a football game in college and lost, he knew that his future was in jeopardy. To stop the hassle from his creditors, he dropped out of school to get away from it all. His mediocre jobs did not provide him with a reasonable income, so he began to gamble again. Now, older and more sophisticated, he began to steal to cover his debts. When, in utter desperation, he walked into a bank and demanded money, he was arrested and went to jail to ponder all that might have been.

His story is not unique, of course, but what does set Jeff apart is that he was raised in a fine Christian home and a good church. He did not begin to gamble because he was hungry or because his parents had neglected him. It all began in good fun, and it offered a bit of relief from boredom. Early on, Jeff felt called to be a pastor or even a missionary; he was in college to prepare for seminary. The contrast between what might have been and what was makes the story all the more painful.

Gambling can capture the heart of anyone, whether non-Christian or Christian; parishioner or pastor. Many people who never thought they would be snared by this lure are secretly coping with this curse, this debilitating habit that corrodes families and churches. Not only is this curse spreading in our society, it is sponsored by our governments and some churches.

What is gambling? It is "an activity in which a person subjects something of value—usually money—to risk involving a large element of chance in hope of winning something of greater value, which is usually more money."[1] In recent years the gambling industry has preferred to call it "gaming" to give it a better image.

Years ago the church took a stand against gambling; today we hear nary a word. I cannot paint the picture too bleak: just ask the children whose parents have divorced because of gambling losses; just ask the child whose mother spends a hundred dollars a week on lottery tickets rather than buying clothes and food. In a word, gambling destroys families.

The purpose of this chapter is to answer several questions about gambling. Is it just harmless entertainment, or is it a sin? What is the profile of the addict? And finally, is there hope for those who know they are addicted and want out? And what are the consequences of those who are addicted but won't admit it?

## IS GAMBLING HARMLESS ENTERTAINMENT?

Why should those of us who do not gamble care about what others do with their spare time and money? Are not those who oppose gambling moralists, in the habit of making "much ado about nothing"? Millions of people gamble without becoming addicted, and that's their business; sure, it involves risk, but so does crossing a street. And, besides, many states now receive heavy revenues used for education from the gambling industry. Why complain?

But if we care about our nation's families, we have to be very concerned about the proliferation of gambling in society. Gambling is not just the pastime of adults, but teenagers and even children are being targeted to be captured in this snare. James Dobson writes, "Studies show that about two-thirds of teens have gambled this past year.

Sometimes they are betting on sports or cards with their friends, but a staggering percentage are gambling on legal activities despite their ages. In Massachusetts, 47 percent of seventh-graders and three-quarters of high school seniors, have played the lottery. . . . In a survey of 12,000 Louisiana adolescents, one-quarter reported playing video poker, 17 percent had gambled on slot machines and one in ten had bet on horse or dog racing."[2] In Connecticut, 24 percent of high school children had cut classes to gamble.

Parents, are you listening?

What kind of an effect did gambling have on these young people? In the Massachusetts high school study, one in twenty had already been arrested for gambling-related offenses; 10 percent had family problems related to gambling; and 8 percent had gotten into trouble at work or school because of gambling. Two-thirds of the hard-core gamblers in detention admitted stealing specifically to finance their gambling.[3]

The statistics could go on. In Michigan, 45 percent of male college football and basketball players admit to gambling on sports, despite rules explicitly prohibiting those activities. More than 5 percent admit to shaving points, leaking inside information for gambling purposes, or betting on their own games. About 8 percent of teens are already hooked on gambling. The *Chicago Tribune* reports: "Young gamblers steal, sell drugs, poach their parents' credit cards, embezzle from employers, sell belongings and even commit suicide when caught up in their addiction."[4]

An alderman here in Chicago told me that he estimates that $100,000 leaves his district on paydays, due to gambling. This is money that should be spent on clothes, food, and rent. Pity the children living in squalor because the father believes that playing the lottery will be his "ticket out."

Throughout the 1990s gambling was legalized in state after state, as lawmakers sought ways to raise money for schools and public works projects. Our own Chicago mayor has defended gambling with the phrase "Jobs, jobs, jobs," but is this a valid reason for establishing a gambling community? For one thing, no civilized nation should build the economy on the backs of those who are being exploited, those who exchange money for an elusive promise of becoming rich at someone else's expense. For another, gambling, far from earning the state money, actually costs it money since so much is spent to control the other crimes that gambling spawns.

A 1982 article in *Psychology Today* talks about the destructiveness of psychological gambling, noting that Dr. Robert Politzer, an expert on compulsive gambling, "estimates that each compulsive gambler disrupts the lives of 10 to 17 others." And because the gambler "usually bets twice what he makes, [he] costs society approximately $40,000 a year."[5]

The National Council on Problem Gambling says that one in five pathological gamblers attempt suicide. Off-duty police Sgt. Solomon Bell, after losing thousands of dollars in a Detroit casino, tried one last hand of blackjack, and lost. The *Chicago Tribune* reported, "The officer stood, cried out 'Nooooo!' drew his gun and put a bullet in his head as other gamblers scrambled for safety."[6] Friends said the thirty-eight-year-old officer was a jovial person with few visible problems. His record was unblemished, but the losses were too much for him.

Senior adults are also being lured into the market. Casinos are seducing an alarming number of seniors, hoping to capitalize on their free time and extra money. Many of the seniors return every week to recover the savings they lost through gambling.

There the elderly enter into a self-contained fantasy world of glittering lights, mirrored columns, and crystal chandeliers. "The buzzers, bells, flashing lights, and clanging of tokens dropping into the slot machine trays can be mesmerizing in an environment with no windows or clocks."[7]

Casinos hire tour companies to arrange low-cost trips to gather senior citizens from various areas and bring them to the nearest casino. For example, some 9 million people a year are brought to Atlantic City by casino buses, and Sunday is their busiest day of the week. Many seniors who have been lured by the fantasy are ashamed to come back to church. There are some six hundred casinos in twenty-six states.

Pat Fowler, executive director of the Orlando-based Florida Council on Compulsive Gambling, asks: "Who else will pick you up at your home, take you to engage in an exciting activity in a safe environment, give you lunch, call you by your name, and make you feel important? Our society sees seniors primarily as disposable, and this industry has picked up on that."[8] A casino in Iowa gives older club members a 50 percent discount on prescription drugs. Some casinos give the elderly a card that keeps track of wins and losses; you might qualify for a free meal or hotel room. Many of the patrons are women who use gambling as an escape to relieve boredom, loneliness, and depression.

We should also be concerned about gambling because it appeals to the basest of human motives; it fuels the sin of greed discussed in the previous chapter. As such it is based on false advertising. Lotteries advertise, "Play today, cash tonight," or, "The shortest route to easy street." Here in a Chicago ghetto, a casino advertisement read, "This could be your ticket out!" Of course the ads feature the lure of the good life, luxury, and pleasure. This is appealing, particularly to the poor, who can least afford the tickets.

Some of us remember when gambling was not just strictly regulated, but forbidden. We might have understood if the government had tolerated it, but no one would have dreamed that the government would become part of the gambling business. We can hardly imagine the government getting into the pornography business (though given our moral decline, anything is possible), but today the government has not only legalized gambling but is sponsoring it. Government sponsorship lessens the stigma attached to gambling; indeed, today it appears as if buying a lottery ticket is a civic responsibility. After all, you are helping to support your community.

Lottery administrators know that patrons no longer get excited at the prospect of winning a few million dollars; therefore greater prizes are needed to bring in the money. Do you remember the craze over the $295 million Powerball jackpot? Some students gambled their tuition money and some homemakers used their grocery money. When the Social Security checks arrive, people line up to play the lotto, expecting to turn their small income into great wealth.

Of course there are many ways to gamble. Since 1995, Internet users have been able to gamble on one or more of the 140 unregulated Web sites where participants can rack up thousands of dollars of credit card debt with a few keystrokes. Indeed, many people are losing their savings by buying stocks and bonds "on line" and with the click of a mouse have turned their computers into casinos. Even paramutual betting on horses, dogs, and the like is still popular, but perhaps the most popular form of gambling is the state lottery, now in thirty-seven states.

According to the International Gaming and Wagering Business, Americans lost $50 billion in legal games in 1997—about $27 billion in casinos and $16 billion in lotteries. The statistics for the year 2000 are even higher. Although many people control the amount they spend, others find that the compulsion is difficult to overcome. The more they lose, the stronger their desire to win their money back.

## IS GAMBLING A SIN?

At least some of the blame for the explosion in gambling opportunities must be laid at the door of the church. The one pillar of society that should stand against gambling is either silent or embraces it. "The biggest things we have to help people are churches and temples and government. And now they are all in the gambling business," said anti-gambling activist Arnie Wexler.[9]

Is gambling entertainment, a sin, or just a weakness? Is it all right to gamble in moderation since there are many who never become addicted? There is no eleventh commandment that says, "Thou shalt not gamble." The Catholic Church has always sanctioned gambling if it is not done to an extreme. When the late Cardinal Bernadin of Chicago suggested that the churches should raise their funds through gifts rather than bingo, he raised a firestorm of controversy. Many complained that without gambling the church could not reach its budget.

George Washington is quoted as saying, "Gambling is the child of avarice, the brother of iniquity, and the father of mischief." Yet we are told he kept a detailed account of his own winnings and losses in card games. Augustine was right when he said, "The Devil invented gambling," and, thankfully, as far as I know, unlike Washington, he practiced what he preached.

I agree with Augustine. I believe the devil invented gambling, and therefore it is a sin. Although the Bible does not speak to the issue directly, let's consider some principles I think would lead us to that conclusion.

## The Violation of the Work Ethic

Gambling ridicules work as a means to obtain money. One gambling ad said there are two ways to earn a million dollars: one is to work hard and the other is to gamble. You are a fool, the argument goes, to go to work each day when you could win a million dollars in the lotto. Yet Paul wrote, "If a man will not work, he shall not eat" (2 Thessalonians 3:10). Work is both a command and a gift of God (Exodus 20:9; Ephesians 4:28; 2 Thessalonians 3:6–12).

Biblically, there are only four ways to obtain money. The first is work; the second, as an inheritance; the third, from investments; and the fourth, as a gift. Gambling does not fall into any of those categories. Gambling is stealing from others to become rich; it thrives on human weakness. "Gambling," someone has said, "is a parasite that feeds on individuals and society."

Of course someone might object, saying that gambling isn't stealing since people give their money "voluntarily" when they wager their bets. True, but it is something like taking money from a drunk; he might "give" it to you, but do you have the right to take it? Remember, the people who "gave" it to you did not do so because they cared about you; they cared about themselves and really wanted what you got. They gave it with the greedy expectation that they would hit the jackpot, but by chance you did instead. They gave with the basest of motives—the same motives with which you bought your ticket. If you should happen to win the lottery, you have in your hand someone else's grocery money; someone else's clothing money; someone else's retirement money.

Gambling is stealing by mutual consent. Because people agree to do something does not make it moral.[10] Yes, there is some risk investing in the stock market, but it is based on real earnings and the essential stability of the economy. Investing in companies based on potential growth is one thing; submitting one's wager to the roll of the dice is another.

## The Misuse of Stewardship

Jesus told a story about a king who called ten of his servants and gave them each a mina, or talent of money. His orders were, "Put this money to work . . . until I come back" (Luke 19:13). When the king returned and asked for an accounting, all of the servants except one had used their money well. The delinquent servant, however, had not used his money to gain more. "Sir, here is your mina; I have kept it laid away in a piece of cloth. I was afraid of you, because you are a hard man. You take out what you did not put in and reap where you did not sow" (vv. 20–21).

The king was not amused. He berated the servant, "You wicked servant! . . . Why then didn't you put my money on deposit, so that when I came back, I could have collected it with interest?" (vv. 22–23). Then the king commanded that his talent be taken from him, and evidently the lazy man was put to death. Give the servant credit for keeping his talent hidden in the earth; at least he had something to offer the king! Think of what the king would have had to say if the wicked man had lost his one talent through gambling!

This, by the way, is the answer to those who say, "I gamble, but only a fixed amount. I just buy two lottery tickets a week and no more." The amount of money wagered does not change the essential nature of gambling. Small stakes gambling is a difference of degree, not kind.[11] Many people participate in "charity gambling," that is, gambling to support a school or a church. But if you want to support such a charity, why not give the money directly?

## Dissatisfaction with God's Provision

Sitting in a dungeon, Paul wrote, "I know what it is to be in need, and I know what it is to have plenty. I have learned the secret of being content in any and every situation, whether well fed or hungry, whether living in plenty or in want. I can do everything through him who gives me strength" (Philippians 4:12–13). Gambling appeals to greed, what Bill Hybels calls "the monster called 'more.'" Gambling is based on the "itch to be rich."

We are to direct our faith toward God to supply what we need. Belief in God's providence and belief in "luck" are two different things, two mutually exclusive objects of faith. Paganism has always appealed to luck; Christians appeal to God.

But can't God control the role of the dice? Does not the Bible speak of the "casting of lots"? Yes, lots were "cast" in Old Testament times, but this was only sanctioned in those instances where the people were deciding on a yes or no answer about decisions that needed to be made. Lots were never used with God's approval to gamble about money. The soldiers who cast lots for Christ's robe violated this biblical teaching and are not an example for us to follow!

Some people buy a lottery ticket and then pray they will win, arguing, quite correctly, that God has the outcome of the lottery in His providential hands. Yes, of course, God could make you or me the winner, but think of how many others would lose! Even the Almighty could not arrange that everyone receive his money back (short of creating money ex nihilo, of course!). Since the gambler refuses to be a wise steward of God's resources, it seems that God has no reason to regard his prayer. Yes, all of life is a risk, but gambling is an artificially contrived risk, with the winner's gain directly related to the loser's loss.

## Gambling and Other Sins

The sin of gambling often brings other sins with it. The shame caused by losses brings secrecy and deception. The desire to "win my money back" leads to borrowing or to the selling of valuable items. Wherever the goddess of money appears, morality is quickly compromised. Dostoyevsky was right when he said, "Gambling and superstition go hand in hand." A wise man wrote, "He who works his land will have abundant food, but he who chases fantasies lacks judgment" (Proverbs 12:11). *Chasing fantasies!*

Gambling stands against everything that is decent, honorable, and biblical. The gambling industry has no fear of the church, no fear of the religious community and its committed opposition.

Let us hear it again from the mouth of the Lord: "He who works his land will have abundant food, but he who chases fantasies lacks judgment." Gambling incites fantasies of the most damaging sort. Gambling and crime are based on the same premise: that we have the right to receive something for nothing.

## TOURING THE MIND OF AN ADDICT

What turns an occasional gambler into a compulsive one? For some, it begins with a traumatic change of lifestyle and the search for an escape, a quick fix. Seniors are particularly vulnerable after the death of a loved one or the loneliness of a new environment. Loneliness drives them to seek some excitement, and of course they think they have the stamina and experience to resist the lure of a gambling compulsion. After a few times, despite their losses, they find themselves entering that dark, yet exciting, world of gambling. For a time they can forget their concerns and enter a bubble of euphoria and privacy. Unfortunately, when they lose everything, they cannot start over again.

Gambling takes decent people and makes them compromise their cherished convictions. People who have not had a past criminal record find themselves writing bad checks or stealing money from relatives. We've all known people who have gambled away their savings, their homes, their income. One man lost it all in a single weekend. With nine out of eleven bets turning sour, his double or nothing bail-out wager on a Houston Oilers–New York Giants game left him owing $46,000 to a bookie he'd never met.[12]

Losses bring gamblers to shame; a kind of shame that makes them try to hide their problem, often with drink or even suicide. The depression of mounting debts and the memory of what they once had weighs heavily upon their minds. In a rescue mission 18 percent said that gambling was the cause of their homelessness.

Some 4 percent of people in America are addicted to gambling. These people have felt the shame of losing, the guilt of knowing how they might have spent their money. But they will not stop their habit. They are the ones who go into debt to "even the score," telling themselves that if they ever win their money back, they will never gamble again. They are quite confident that given enough tries, and enough money, they will win it all back. To quit now is to admit defeat; it is to leave money in the system; it is to live with the knowledge that someone else is enjoying their "investments." Yes, they want to get it all back, but they are chasing a fantasy.

Those who try to help an addict must understand that he does not operate on the basis of normal reasoning; he has his own form of reasoning that makes perfectly good sense to him. His addiction changes the way he sees the world. He looks at all of life through a bent lens. All the discussion in the world will probably not change him; only a severe dose of reality can do that.

## A Mood Change

The addict, like the rest of us, is seeking happiness, or at least peace of soul. He needs a way of escape, and his addiction gives him euphoria and a sense of "being in control." When he practices his addiction, it is as if he is in a trance; he can live in two worlds simultaneously, the real world and the world of his giddy elation. "Oh, it's great," said one addict. "It's wonderful, especially when you get the money in your hands. It's something for nothing. You never think of losing. Losing isn't an option." However, as he discovered, losing might not be an option, but it is a reality.

The gambling addict experiences an incredible rush of euphoria when he puts a high bet on a his favorite football team's chance of winning by six points. As the time comes for the game to be on television he is in ecstasy, anticipating the excitement and the possibility of the big win. It doesn't happen, of course, so later he is plunged into the depths of despair from which only another gambling "rush" will rescue him.

## A Defense System

Early on, the addict begins to build his defense system to protect himself from those who would attempt to rid him of this fantasy. He arms himself with lies, half-truths, and manipulative strategies to make sure that no one will ever rid him of his emotional buzz. Now he becomes convinced that others do not understand him, and he cannot unburden himself, for it would bring him shame. Even friends would not understand and would try to rid him of his most precious means of escape.

Keep in mind that the addict's need for his "fix" grows ever more urgent. Everytime he gambles, has a drink, or has sex, his "high" is soon deflated. He is left with the sadness and shame of realizing that his secret habit has not brought the peace that he wanted. This "let down" puts him in a state of despair that only his addiction can cure; so he participates again, only to experience a greater low. Only a bigger bet, more drink, or a more risqué experience can re-create his "rush." As his losses become greater, superstition and magic begin to replace his better judgment. He is in love with an illusion.

## The Fantasy of Security

An addiction can be defined as a pathological love and trust relationship with an object or event. The addict rejoices in the knowledge that this object or event will always be there when he needs it. People may disappoint him; the church might fail him; his family might turn away from him. But the casino will still be there, or the breathless excitement he receives when he bets on a football game will return when he needs it.

What follows now is important: Because everything is now interpreted through the lens of his particular object or event, he will begin to treat people just as he treats his alcoholism or gambling. Because he has been able to manipulate these objects or events for his own pleasure, he will begin to manipulate people the same way. They will exist only in relationship to his habit. Because they do not fall in line with him, he will begin to distrust people and trust only his own addiction, despite its failed promises.

The addict will shift blame, shade the truth, lie, and intimidate those around him. Meanwhile, people will try to reason with him, tell him that he has a problem, and urge him to quit. But in his mind, it is *they* who have a problem. His distorted view of reality will be the means by which he will now judge others.

All meaningful relationships with others are therefore jeopardized, so the addict becomes increasingly isolated. Along with his distrust, he is angry that everyone does not see his point of view. Thus his world is internalized; it becomes a place from which vantage point everything is now interpreted. His world will become increasingly more secretive, more isolated, more necessary.

Ending a gambling addiction is not easy. Again, let us look at this through the eyes of the addict. He does not know of anything that gives him the same thrill as gambling; there is a euphoria that he gets as he buys his ticket, puts money into the slot machine, or gambles on his favorite team. The thought of leaving all of this behind is an unthinkable thought, seemingly beyond his ability.

He cannot bear the thought that he has squandered the money he so dearly loves and needs. He gambles because he loves money, yet gambling causes him to lose what is precious to him. Do you see the bind he is in? He thinks back to the $200 he lost at the casino; he knows he was a fool to lose it, so he needs to win it back to save face with his family and particularly with himself. He's determined to reclaim it in order to live with himself.

Perhaps the gambler's most enduring fantasy is that he honestly believes that the more times he tries to win in gambling, the better his chances! In fact, some think that a loss just means that he is more likely to get lucky the next time! But that is a lie. Think of it this way: the more lottery tickets one buys, the better probability one has that one will win the jackpot. But after the drawing has taken place, the faithful gambler does *not* have a better shot at winning the next time around! His probability reverts back to the same number it is for the first-time gambler! *He does not realize that increasing the number of gambling experiences does not increase the probability that he will win.*

All of these cherished notions must be shattered before the gambler is ready to quit. Since he is essentially a selfish person who does not care about the impact his habit has on anyone else, he will not change his ways until reality breaks into his life. As long as he still has some money in the bank; as long as he can still pay the rent; as long as his lights are still on in the house; as long as he has food in his stomach, he will continue his addiction.

## HOW SANITY RETURNS

What will cause the gambler to seek help? What will finally turn him around?

## The Power of Truth

Jesus taught that the truth sets us free. For some, this reality does not settle in until they have lost their house, their family, or their spouse. When the house must be sold, when the retirement account no longer exists, when creditors come to take the furniture—only then will some say with King Saul of the Old Testament, "Surely I have acted like a fool and have erred greatly" (1 Samuel 26:21). Yes, the addict needs to be set free, and only the truth can do it.

Whatever the addiction, the addict must hit bottom, but concerned friends can "raise the bottom," helping the addict to see the truth before the divorce happens or the mortgage on the house is foreclosed. This can be done in a group setting, each member of the family telling the addict how his habit affects them. His insulated world must be penetrated. A life does not have to be ruined before it can be repaired.

Years ago, a professor of theology called me to confess the sin of gambling. He, like others, had tried to hide his losses, but his wife discovered the high amounts on the credit cards—a total of $30,000, to be exact. His elaborate scheme of deception came unraveled, and now he had to admit the truth. His wife was devastated, wondering if she could ever trust her husband again. But after some counseling and a commitment to the marriage, they mortgaged their house and began to repay the losses. Eventually, their financial situation stabilized, and they were able to restore their relationship. As long as this man's vice was secret, he maintained his compulsive behavior; but when his cover was blown, he ended his gambling career. Most are not that fortunate.

One man I know quit gambling after an inheritance given to him by his parents was secretly squandered. When the lights were turned out, when his wife threatened to leave and his friends were angry with him because he owed them money—that was the wake-up call, a reminder that it was time to quit gambling. The devil does his most shameful work in secret; consequently, exposure often is necessary for change to take place. The humility of asking for help is important.

## The Intervention of Christ

If the addict has never trusted Christ personally for salvation, this would be a wonderful time to remind him of the promise "Yet to all who received him, to those who believed in his name, he gave the right to become children of God—children born not of natural descent, nor of human decision or a husband's will, but born of God" (John 1:12–13). If he already is a believer, his sin must be confessed, with the assurance that God will forgive him and "cleanse [him] from all unrighteousness" (1 John 1:9 KJV).

Keep in mind that the recovering addict not only hates himself but thinks that God hates him, too. The feelings of disgust for what he has done are believed to be God-given. Only when he senses that he has been restored to God will he be able to face the task of being restored to those whom he has betrayed. Once the addict has accepted the truth, this is not the time to berate him for what he has done; he knows all too well that he has failed everyone. He needs to be given the hope of restoration, forgiveness, and emotional healing.

Also remember that what drove the addict to his secret addiction was an inner emptiness; there was that feeling of loneliness that the addiction seemed to fill. Thus, the addict must develop his relationship with God and his friends, realizing that in our nearness to God and His people our souls find solace and strength.

## The Need for Restoration

Since it is impossible to repent in this one area of life and not another, it is essential that the gambler confess all the sins that the addiction spawned: lying, cheating, greed, and the like. He must go to those who have been affected by his sin and ask their forgiveness too. God always stands ready to forgive and deliver people from their sins when they finally allow Him to inspect every area of their lives. The more complete the repentance, the more sure the deliverance.

Once the addict responds in humility to the truth, there has to be a plan of restoration, an agreement as to what has to be done with past debts and how the future is to be managed. I've had more than one gambler say, "I promise I'll quit as soon as I win it all back."

If that is his response, he has to be asked how: How will you feel when you have lost twice the money you have lost now? Losing more money is not the answer to make up for money already lost.

The fact that money has been wasted must simply be humbly accepted. Consider it tuition for having learned the hard way that "he who chases fantasies lacks judgment" (Proverbs 12:11). If there has to be a repayment plan for outstanding loans, this needs to be factored into the equation. There is no easy way out of the quicksand, but as long as the gambling stops, at least there are limits to how much further the gambler can sink.

## The Need for Accountability

Finally, whenever possible there must be controls placed on money. The gambler cannot be allowed to have use of funds without accountability. Despite all the promises to the contrary, the addict is always tempted to re-create his exciting world, thinking that the "big win" is out there somewhere. He is still ashamed of his losses; he still thinks that if he could win a windfall, he would finally restore his sense of dignity. The lie he once believed will come back, wanting to be believed once more.

Most communities where gambling is permitted have hot lines to help those who wish to be free from their gambling addiction. But few people call because they are too ashamed to seek help. Gamblers Anonymous (GA), begun in 1957, has helped thousands of people "kick the habit." Just like alcoholics, many gamblers who attend for a few months think they have conquered their vice, only to have a relapse. The hold of gambling is so strong that only about 8 percent of those who attend are able to stop gambling even after attending GA for two years. One gambler who has attended for thirty-two years says, "This compulsion took my very soul and made me a slave." New members are assigned a sponsor who has the responsibility of follow-up. Those who seek help by surrender to God and the authority of the church fare much better. Ultimately, God is the one who can cleanse the heart from guilt and give the fallen a new motivation for living. God replaces the darkness with light and gives the weak strength.

## A PRAYER TO BEGIN THE JOURNEY

*Father, I thank You for showing me the idolatry of gambling; I admit I have looked to luck to supply my physical and emotional needs. I repent of the sin of gambling, knowing that this was never Your plan for me. Forgive me for the misuse of the funds You have given me. I rebuke Satan, who has made me doubt Your promises; I have believed the lie that I had a right to get rich quick, without due process.*

*I accept any consequences of my habit as discipline for my waywardness. By Your grace I will ask forgiveness of those I have wronged and, where possible, make restitution. Most of all, I ask for Your forgiveness and grace. Today, I give You my future, resting in the confidence that You will take care of me.*

*Help me to make any sacrifice You ask that I might be free of this curse. My confidence is in Jesus, who was sent "to proclaim freedom for the prisoners and recovery of sight for the blind, to release the oppressed, to proclaim the year of the Lord's favor" (Luke 4:18–19). Today, I accept this promise as mine.*

*In Jesus' name, Amen.*

# ALCOHOLISM: QUITTING TOMORROW

*T*here is a story about a man who would buy four beers every time he visited the bar. He explained that he had three brothers in Europe and they had made an agreement that whenever they drank, they would drink a beer for each other. "Just one for each of us," he explained. But one day this patron came in, sat on a barstool, and ordered only *three* beers. The bartender was sympathetic, suspecting that one of the man's brothers had died. "Oh, no," he said, "it's just that *I've* quit drinking."

We smile at the story, but all of us know that alcoholism is no laughing matter. Everyone reading these lines knows someone whose life has been destroyed because of alcohol; and, since no one lives in isolation, families and even distant relatives have felt the ill effects. No one can calculate the grief, shame, and poverty alcohol and drug dependence have brought to our nation and to our churches. This is perhaps one of the most widespread "secret snares."

We can be thankful that in recent years the media has highlighted the personal struggles of celebrities such as former first lady Betty

Ford, the late Mickey Mantle, and actress Elizabeth Taylor. This exposure has helped bring alcoholism out of the closet so that it can be discussed and remedied. Yet millions suffer in silence, not knowing where to turn. The alcoholic refuses to get help, and his or her dependents must submit to the code of silence.

## DISPELLING THE MYTHS

The myth that only certain people with a genetic propensity toward alcoholism are prone to becoming addicts must be exposed. I'm not denying that some people have a genetic tendency toward addiction. In a previous chapter I mentioned that adopted children whose birth parents are alcoholics have been shown to have a tendency to turn to alcoholism even if they are brought up in a home with parents who do not drink. But that is only part of the story.

The other part of the story is that many people who supposedly have no such genetic disposition have fallen victim to the goddess of alcohol. They are particularly vulnerable if they have suffered some loss or a feeling of loneliness or disappointment. Or perhaps they were emotionally, physically, or sexually abused as children. Addictions grow best in the soil of ruptured family relationships. Feelings of rejection and shame are so powerful that it seems natural to seek a way to cope, a way to deaden the raw pain of emotional depression.

If you were raised in a family that lacked close nurturing relationships; or in a dysfunctional family where a parent's alcoholism forced you to stuff your feelings into your soul; or in a family where the code of silence was operative, where the truth about life could never be discussed, then you have a greater potential for addiction. "Genetic propensity" matters little when emotional survival is at stake. Even those who grew up with an aversion toward alcohol have turned to the bottle when the depression seemed unbearable.

The bottom line is that any one of us could become an addict. Research repeatedly shows that a certain percentage of people who participate in social drinking will turn out to be alcoholics. Many who come from good families, many whose biological parents did not drink, many who had a happy childhood have turned to the bottle in times of distress. We cannot predict in advance who might succumb and who might not. Craig Nakken was right when he said, "The foundation of the addict is found in all people. It's found in a normal desire to make it through life with the least amount of pain and the greatest amount of pleasure possible."[1]

We have an innate desire to avoid pain and live a life of happiness. This desire is right and good and lies deeply embedded in the hearts of all of us. The addict thinks that he has found a way to avoid sadness; his addiction makes the promise that, if it is followed, there will be fulfillment, a feeling of "aliveness." The addiction gives the feeling of escape without the need to feel the harsh pain of reality, for the euphoria of alcohol will replace it. Pia Mellody has defined addiction as "any process used to avoid or take away intolerable reality."[2]

There is no reason for self-righteousness on the matter of addiction. It is a danger for me; it is a danger for you. When the snare is laid, we can be caught and our lives ruined. Addiction knows no boundaries of class, gender, or vocation. Millions of men are addicted; so are millions of women and teenagers. Members of the clergy, doctors, attorneys, and accountants have chemical dependency. Just recently a minister was found to have an alcohol addiction that led him to justify impropriety of every kind, including fraud. Although the Bible does not teach abstinence, given our penchant for taking the path of least resistance, abstinence from alcohol appears to be a wise policy.

A second myth is that all of the addicts end up on skid row as homeless beggars on the street. No, there are millions of addicts, and they are found functioning in every vocation and level of society. Addicts go to work each day, carry out their needed responsibilities, and return to their families only to drown their woes by abusing some substance, such as alcohol or drugs.

A family told me how their father would serve others all day in the ministry, eat dinner, drink to his fill, sleep it off, and go to work the next day and disciple others in the Christian life. I've known students who abused drugs, if not every day, then every weekend, went to class, studied, and passed their exams. But hidden beneath their lives in the real world was another world of booze and drugs. They were able to move from one world to another without too many people finding out.

There are millions of functioning alcoholics. In fact, the reason they are not seeking help is precisely because they can function well enough to get by. So they tell themselves that they are well in control of their habit. But they lie.

## THE PATH TO
## ALCOHOL AND DRUG ADDICTION

What are those steps in becoming addicted? These steps do not necessarily happen in sequence. They might evolve in a reverse order, or they might develop together. If we understand the path the addict has taken, we will be in a better position to help him retrace his steps and find the way out.

Addiction always begins with that first drink, that first shot of cocaine. Experimenting with the substance produces a mood change. By gorging himself with food, the glutton feels a sense of control; there is the promise of fulfillment, a promise of happiness, a belief that the addiction will help to eliminate the pain.

Alcohol or drugs create a sense of euphoria. Those who are "high" on drugs or "wasted" with alcohol experience what could best be described as a "euphoric trance." There is a pleasurable sensation that detaches the participant from the pain of reality, creating a whole new world. The participant can traverse between this unreal world and the real world without anyone else really knowing it. No wonder one mind-altering drug is called *ecstasy*.

That first intoxication experience can lead to an immediate and profound mood change. Many alcoholics can describe in detail their first drinking experience; the gambler can recall the euphoria of either winning a bet or knowing someone who did. The drug addict can recall the first few powerful highs that made him confident this was the escape to happiness. No matter how people disappoint him; no matter how he is mistreated, shouted at, or misunderstood, there is a world he can access, a world that holds out the promise of happiness and escape. In fact, the very thought of participating in that next "fix" creates shortness of breath and a sensation that runs through the entire body.

Second, there is a transfer of faith to the substance. Perhaps the addict has always believed in God or has had a decent relationship with other people. But both God and his friends have disappointed him. Now he no longer needs them, for he has a sure substitute that will not disappoint. He has confidence that his bottle will work every time, lifting him into that other world where he feels confident and successful. The crack cocaine addict has faith that this substance will always be his savior, lifting him to heights of elation where the problems of life are forgotten or marginalized. He cannot depend on people because his relationships have soured, but he can depend on his substance. At least one thing in this world is secure.

Put yourself in the shoes of many of today's teenagers. Life is cruel. Your family might be dysfunctional; perhaps illness has struck one of your parents; and, of course, there are financial struggles. You have found difficulties in your romantic relationships. You feel guilty for sexual indulgence, and now you also feel rejected and want to "loosen up" so that you can enjoy yourself. You are in an environment where everyone around you is drinking; it is the way of life on the college campus. In the safety of friends who are looking for the same escape as you, you can trust the bottle to give you that feeling of well-being. Based on past experience, it will escort you into the world of guaranteed pleasure and give you acceptance at the same time. What a discovery! God is distant; people are fickle, and life is filled with sorrow, but the bottle or your drug of choice will be there to do its work.

A college student claimed that she drank almost every night, followed by sex with a man she scarcely knew. To quote her words exactly, "When you wake up in the morning you say to yourself, 'What I did wasn't so bad because I was drunk and didn't know what I was doing.'" Think of all that drink did for her: it made her loosen up, it helped drown her guilt, it made her popular with the boys—and, what is more, it will be there for her again tomorrow! Immorality without responsibility! Euphoria without guilt! That's more than God could do for her!

But of course when we transfer our trust from God to the substance we break the first commandment: "You shall have no other gods before me" (Exodus 20:3). When a substance takes the place of God, it becomes an idol, and the Scriptures teach that Satan stands behind idols, reinforcing their power and enhancing their appeal to our flesh. During those moments of exhilaration, the attachment to the substance grows. There is a bonding that develops between the person and the substance.

With this bonding comes a loss of control. The participant now begins to surrender his life to the substance in exchange for the promise of future escape and exhilaration. Life is not as painful as it once was, and the future can be faced with more confidence and the knowledge that at any time this new world can be created. The pains of life can be forgotten and happiness gained. But as his tolerance for alcohol increases, he must drink more to get the same effect.

But unlike God, these substances do not keep their promises. After the euphoria has passed, the emptiness and depression begins. Reentry into the real world is accompanied by a sense of shame and regret, a feeling that one has been belittled. The longer the developing addict ponders what he has done, the more he is overwhelmed by a sense of shame and regret. He curses the bottle, for it has deceived him. He knows he has been cheated of the sense of accomplishment and completeness he felt when he faced the difficulties of life without this security blanket.

The emotional pain gnaws on him, but he does not know where to turn for help. The thought of living with this emptiness is depressing. He has only one attractive recourse, and that is to alter his mood by submitting once again to his substance of choice. He asks the bottle to repeat the promise that he will drift into the "other world," but later the promise fails. Shame begets more shame. *He drinks to solve the problems caused by drinking.*

Thus, the addict enters the world of delusion. "Slowly, over time, addictive logic develops into a belief system—a delusion system from which the addicted person's life will be directed."[3] This delusion becomes all-consuming and from now on will dictate all of his decisions. His addiction will be the hub, the very center of his life, and all the spokes will have to find their place in relationship to it. The purpose of life will now be redirected: sustaining the addiction will be the chief focus of his waking moments. Mel Trotter, who became a Christian leader, used to tell about his days of alcoholism prior to his conversion. He tiptoed into a funeral parlor and stole the little shoes from his dead infant's feet to sell them for another drink.

Third, there is the development of a protective shell, which is needed to sustain the addiction. The purpose of this shell is twofold: First, so that the addict can sink more deeply into his own world of fantasy and ecstasy. Second, to keep people out, to make sure that no one is going to disrupt his mood changes. Since shame is more powerful than physical pain, this defensive wall will insure that he will minimize the possibility that he will be exposed for what he is. So you don't like his addiction? It doesn't matter. He can live without your blessing, acceptance, or approval. Say what you like, his drug will be there for him, creating his rapturous world.

Now, occasionally a crack might develop in this protective shell. A ray of light will flash upon his soul, or perhaps he will wake up with such a sense of regret that he honestly believes he must "come clean." But within a few days, the flicker will be extinguished, and a dark delusion will settle over his soul and he will be back to square one.

Those who live with such an addict will find it difficult or even impossible to maintain a meaningful relationship with him. To reason with him is to be embroiled in a series of arguments and rationalizations. His moods will simply have to be accepted, since there is little use in trying to help him see life from a different perspective. To live with himself, his protective shell must become thicker, less prone to cracks and vulnerabilities. From now on, everyone exists for only one purpose—to help maintain his way of life.

Friends and family might ask: Why does he act this way? Does he not care about what he is doing to his family? The answer is that he does not care. He sees them only as objects to be manipulated to fit into his way of seeing the world. He does not receive his euphoric experience through his relationship with people; it is his substance that opens the door to exhilarating mood swings.

People (yes, his family) must be sacrificed for the purpose of maintaining the addiction; all moral principles must be laid on the addictive altar. He will tell lies about why he did not go to work and will expect other members of the family to lie for him, too. He will be dishonest about his use of money and crafty in his schemes to defraud others. In fact, his moral compass will become so corroded that he will tell a lie even if telling the truth would serve him better.

This mood-altering world that the substance creates leads to what is called "the addictive personality." We can say that there is his "normal self," with its conscience and moral image, and there is also the "addictive self," with its powerful drives and endless capacity for deception. In Dr. Jekyll and Mr. Hyde this transformation is described: "I was slowly losing hold of my original and better self and becoming slowly incorporated with my second and worse self."[4]

The addict now develops incredible cunning. In order to keep his addiction a secret he will have to think of ways to manipulate people to get the money he will need or to justify himself. There is no end to his deceptions and craftiness. People are to be used as things; they are to serve the one purpose of falling in line with the worldview he is now developing. Such actions seem so reasonable to him that he can't think of why anyone should protest. He is genuinely puzzled as to why others don't see life the way he does.

As he "gets by" with his lifestyle, he might graduate to high-risk behavior, such as grand theft or extortion. If he is a rich alcoholic, such as a doctor or lawyer, he will not have to steal but will, nevertheless, begin to look at his vocation primarily as a way to support his habit. All of life will be interpreted through his narcissistic lens. His care for others will be superficial, for all that matters is the assurance that he can enter his exhilarating world whenever he wishes. The addiction will so distort his vision of reality that it might change the way he views the world for the rest of his life.

To summarize his defense mechanisms:

1. *He will always blame others for his problems.* It will be his employer's fault, his wife's fault, his children's fault, the world's fault, God's fault. He simply will not look into the mirror and confess that it is his fault.

2. *He will become antisocial, and with good reason.* His relationships are frayed because he is critical of everyone in order to justify his aloofness. He will judge people, not by gradations of "goodness," but as either "all good" or "all bad." All of reality will be poured into these two categories. People will either be for him or against him; there is no neutral ground.

3. *He will always create a certain level of chaos to mask his problem.* Normal everyday problems that have a ready solution will be blown out of proportion, so that minor matters are treated as if they are all-consuming. The reason, remember, is not merely so that he can say "life is so difficult," but so that he can distract the focus of those around him to concentrate on these "huge problems" rather than the problem-maker.

4. *He will temporarily quit an addiction to give the illusion that his problem is solved.* Often he will simply switch addictions: he will go from alcohol to overeating or to mood-changing drugs. His addictive personality will continue even if the addiction itself is changed.

## A PATTERN OF FALSE HOPE

There are times when alcoholics can remain sober, often for long periods of time. A cycle is repeated that alternates between hope and despair. Many will go through the throes of recovery but will fall back into familiar patterns.

First, the alcoholic desires to never take another drink. He sees where drink is taking him; he has been shamed once too many times. He is weary of the embarrassment of ruining his family. So he determines, "Never again." And, remarkably, he is successful for a time.

Second, he actually begins to take pride in his sobriety. He tells his friends that he has not had a drink in months. He feels better; he actually has a job again, and everything looks so much brighter. He even has a sense of mastery, telling himself that he has proved that he is not an addict after all—and has been sober several months to prove it.

Third, he takes another drink, confident that he can handle it. This triggers a desire for drink the likes of which he has never experienced. At this point some will go on a two-year binge, drinking with almost no control. "One drink might set the fires of alcoholism to raging out of control in his life. One drink can create an insatiable thirst that will not be quenched. One drink might be enough to plunge him to the very depths of alcoholism as quickly as one can be pushed over a cliff."[5]

He fulfills the words of Scripture, "The evil deeds of a wicked man ensnare him; the cords of his sin hold him fast. He will die for lack of discipline, led astray by his own great folly" (Proverbs 5:22–23). Only painful reality can cause an alcoholic to seek the help he so desperately needs. For many, reality dawns when:

- While cleaning up his vomit left on the kitchen floor the night before, he realizes he must change.
- He looks into the eyes of his children and cannot bear the thought of what he has just done.
- He arrives home and finds that his lights and telephone have been cut off.
- His car is repossessed.
- He is arrested for drunken driving after causing an accident.
- He has just been fired from another job.
- His family leaves him, and his loneliness make him desperate to change.

But, as we have learned, it is possible for the family to help the addict reach the bottom more quickly by intervening in his life. The goal, of course, is to help him see his need before he reaches the absolute bottom.

## BIBLICAL WARNINGS

The Bible has much to say about alcoholism. Although drinking wine was common in the Middle East, even as it is in most parts of the world today, the Bible has many warnings about drunkenness. Here is a summary of its teachings.

First, drunkenness is a judgment of God.

*Woe to those who rise early in the morning to run after their drinks, who stay up late at night till they are inflamed with wine. They have harps and lyres at their banquets, tambourines and flutes and wine, but they have no regard for the deeds of the Lord, no respect for the work of his hands. Therefore my people will go into exile.*

—ISAIAH 5:11–13

Even more clearly, Jeremiah said that God would send the curse of drunkenness to the people as a judgment for their rebellion.

*"This is what the LORD says: I am going to fill with drunkenness*
*all who live in this land, including the kings who sit on*
*David's throne, the priests, the prophets and all those living*
*in Jerusalem. I will smash them one against the other,*
*fathers and sons alike, declares the LORD. I will allow no pity*
*or mercy or compassion to keep me from destroying them."*

—JEREMIAH 13:13–14

Alcoholism is hardly a neutral issue.
Second, drunkenness leads to sorrow.

*Who has woe? Who has sorrow? Who has strife? Who has*
*complaints? Who has needless bruises? Who has bloodshot eyes?*
*Those who linger over wine, who go to sample bowls of mixed*
*wine. Do not gaze at wine when it is red, when it sparkles in the*
*cup, when it goes down smoothly! In the end it bites like a snake*
*and poisons like a viper. Your eyes will see strange sights and*
*your mind imagine confusing things. You will be like one sleep-*
*ing on the high seas, lying on top of the rigging. "They hit me,"*
*you will say, "but I'm not hurt! They beat me, but I don't feel it!*
*When will I wake up so I can find another drink?"*

—PROVERBS 23:29–35

These warnings are for the benefit of those who have not yet begun to drink. No, the Bible does not teach abstinence, so we cannot judge those who drink their glass of wine, but there is only one
way to make sure that we never fall into the sin of alcoholism: simply
refuse to begin drinking. Then even if you have a genetic disposition
toward alcohol you will never rue the day that you had your first drink.

## FINDING A WAY OUT OF THE DARKNESS

For most alcoholics there is not an easy way out of the addiction. Most try to sober up on their own, but they fail because they

do not realize the extent of their need. They underestimate how the years of addiction have skewed their view of themselves, their problem, and even their view of God.

When an alcoholic finally sees himself for who he is, he must also see God for who He is. Both "revelations" often occur simultaneously. God cannot help those who think they can help themselves, but only those who know they cannot help themselves.

David wrote:

> I waited patiently for the Lord; he turned to me and heard my cry. He lifted me out of the slimy pit, out of the mud and mire; he set my feet on a rock and gave me a firm place to stand. He put a new song in my mouth, a hymn of praise to our God. Many will see and fear and put their trust in the LORD.
>
> —PSALM 40:1–3

When David slipped into the "mud and mire," he had a guilty conscience. So in desperation he cried out that God might pick him up and clean him off, figuratively speaking. Only when an alcoholic is weary of sinking into the mud and mire, when he can no longer feel his feet touching the bottom of the slough, is there any hope that he will truly cry to the Lord. For many, admitting they need help is a burden they cannot even imagine. Life without that precious bottle is unthinkable. To face the real world with its harsh realities without being able to transcend into the world of fantasy is more than they can bear.

Yes, there are millions who have been helped through Alcoholics Anonymous with just a belief in a nonspecific "Higher Power." But how much better to be assured that one has been reconciled to the God of the Universe through Christ, who purchased redemption for those who believe! God is able to walk into the addict's life and help him cope with the emptiness that alcohol has left behind.

William Raws of the "House of Mercy" in Whiting, New Jersey, says that those who attempt to conqueror alcoholism with secular programs often discover that the cure is not permanent since the desire for alcohol remains. He has observed that those who put their faith in Christ, memorize Scripture, and are accountable to

Christian leaders have a much better success rate of permanent freedom.[6] The reason is that God does not just change one's behavior but gives the yielded believer new desires that overcome the persistent cravings of the flesh.

Guilt must either be cleansed by God or left to fester, driving its victim further into his addiction. The recovering alcoholic must not only deal with guilt, but shame, the feeling that one has lost his reputation and been disgraced. There are two categories of people: those who experience shame because they have something to be ashamed about, and those who have been shamed. Children of alcoholic parents who have had to abide by the family code of silence but have felt shamed within by the curse that alcohol has brought into their lives have an *acquired shame*. The alcoholic has *direct shame* that reminds him that he personally is guilty and that he is a flawed and defective human being.

John Bradshaw, in his book *Healing the Shame That Binds You,* writes that a shame-based person is haunted by a sense of absence and emptiness: "To be shame bound means that whenever you feel any feeling and need any drive, you immediately feel ashamed."[7] When this shame has been internalized, nothing within you seems to be OK. "To feel shame is to feel seen in an exposed and diminished way."[8] This creates a tormenting self-consciousness.

Filled with shame, an alcoholic is convinced that there is nothing he can do to redeem himself; since all is lost, there is no reason to begin a life of decency. What is more, he generally has been abused and humiliated and therefore feels powerless. So far he has been able to mute the full effects of shame by his mood-altering addiction. For him to let go of his addiction is to face his shame in all of its power and pain. Now without this emotional numbness, he must bear the full brunt of his shame without relief.

Guilt says that I have violated my own values; I have to repair my relationship with God. Specific sins need to be confessed before God, and the guilt will dissipate. But shame is another matter; shame attacks who I am, affirming that I am fundamentally defective; and for that, there must be another cure.

If the answer for guilt is to receive the forgiveness of God, the answer for shame is to receive the acceptance of God. The addict thinks, as all of us do from time to time, "God could never love me, because

I am unworthy of His love." And that is quite true, since we are so unworthy. But remember: God's love is not based on worthiness. As Luther said, God does not love us because we are valuable; we are valuable because He loves us. In other words, God chooses to confer value upon us. Yes, God loves the alcoholic too.

Cleansing by God is the first step toward freedom from alcoholism. For some, coming to know Christ as Savior is an experience of immediate deliverance. For others, the temptation to revert to past behavior is compelling, particularity in times of discouragement and failure. Many an alcoholic has failed with "What's the use, anyway" on his lips.

Second, the alcoholic must come out of hiding. As in the case of the gambling addict, the truth will set him free. As long as the addiction is hidden, it festers and grows. Blessed is the alcoholic who finally is able to share his deep failures and hurt with those who are significant in his life. Here the body of Christ must step in, giving that sense of acceptance and reconciliation that is so desperately needed. The reason that AA has had so much success is because the meetings are filled with fellow travelers who themselves have had the same struggles. There is an immediate identification, a bonding, and a message that comes through loud and clear: You can admit who you are because we have all been there; we stand with you in your shame and sorrow; it is OK to say that you need help. Believers must take an additional step of asking the others for forgiveness for the lies and deception that alcoholism birthed.

Third, there is a desperate need for accountability. This should involve counseling at least once a week, along with the discipline of Scripture memory and gainful employment. If the struggling addict does not have a person whom he can call on the phone when the temptations return; if he does not have someone to pray with him when he is depressed, the temptation becomes more powerful. Close monitoring for at least a year is often necessary. Addicts need a friend who can ask them, "Have you used alcohol this week?" You have to have someone ask you whether you drank this week. "Therefore, strengthen your feeble arms and weak knees. Make level paths for your feet, so that the lame may not be disabled, but rather healed" (Hebrews 12:12).

Fourth, there must be a substitute for the substance abuse: "Do not get drunk on wine, which leads to debauchery. Instead, be filled with the Spirit" (Ephesians 5:18). The Holy Spirit brings wholeness to the individual; the Spirit does what we cannot. Walking in the Spirit is learned as we follow the disciplines of the Christian life.

When we receive Christ as Savior we receive the Holy Spirit within us. Our responsibility is to develop sensitivity to the Spirit, to learn that the Spirit works within us, seeking both our cleansing and faith. "So I say, live by the Spirit, and you will not gratify the desires of the sinful nature" (Galatians 5:16).

Finally, all Christians, particularity addicts, must learn to resist Satan. He uses addictions and our secret desires to detract us from the wholeness Christ intended. He is, after all, the one who makes sin attractive so that we will not fear it. He walks about, stalking us, trying to find a wedge to enter our lives. Yes, there are demons who take the sins of the flesh and strengthen the grip those sins have in our lives.

Satan and his minions must be resisted in the power of Christ. Speaking of Christ, Paul wrote, "He forgave us all our sins, having canceled the written code, with its regulations, that was against us and that stood opposed to us; he took it away, nailing it to the cross. And having disarmed the powers and authorities, he made a public spectacle of them, triumphing over them by the cross" (Colossians 2:13–15).

Today there are thousands of former alcoholics who tell us that life can be different. When we stop focusing on the strength of the sin and focus on the strength of Christ, anyone can be delivered. Yes, this freedom is for alcoholics too.

### A PRAYER TO BEGIN THE JOURNEY

*Father, I confess alcoholism is sin. I admit my helplessness in overcoming it, for I am its slave. I am weary of believing Satan's lies; I am weary of the shame, the secrecy, and the bondage. Today, in Jesus' name, I* rebuke this misuse of my body and mind. Your Word says, "Do not get drunk on wine. . . . Instead, be filled with the Spirit" (Ephesians 5:18). I accept the control of the Spirit, rather than the control of drink. I affirm that as Your child I am loved despite my failures; I rejoice that You love me enough to interrupt my slide into total ruin.

I admit that when I turned to alcohol I not only believed a lie, but lived a lie to cover my sin. Help me to confess and forsake all the sins that accompanied my alcoholism. By Your grace I will be reconciled to the people whose lives I have affected by my sin. Help me to realize that half-hearted repentance is not repentance at all.

I choose to humble myself and seek the help of those who can stand with me against this affliction. By Your grace I will submit myself to their counsel and authority. Grant that repentance might be thorough and long-lasting.

In Jesus' name, Amen.

# PORNOGRAPHY: THE SOUL DEFILED

*O*ur nation is drowning in a sea of sensuality.

Some 70 percent of the time pornography falls into the hands of children, so when a friend of mine was a teenager and found a stash of his father's magazines, he began to browse through the pictures. Though he became a Christian in college, the images stayed with him, and so did his habit. He kept his fantasy world intact, making sure that no one found out about his secret pleasure. He both loved pornography and hated it.

He got married, but communication problems began to develop because he could never be honest and open. Whenever the conversation got too personal, he learned how to steer it toward a more comfortable topic. He knew that if his wife ever found out, she would simply increase his growing sense of shame. When at last his secret came to light and his wife discovered his addiction, she found it difficult to forgive him. She had thought she knew her husband, but this revelation made her realize that she had been living with a man she didn't even know. Thankfully, their marriage recovered when they learned there is hope for addiction and, yes, trust can be rebuilt.

One man with a similar story said, "I lived like a double agent for the CIA, leading two lives. I was actually pretty good at it and thought I would never get caught. But God had been on my trail all along. Now for the first time in my life I am able to be real with others about the junk in my life, not just the good stuff. . . . I am finally living without the constant threat of others finding out who I really am."[1] Yes, this addiction, like others, can only be cured with the truth that sets us free.

There was a time when pornography was confined to adult magazines sold under the counter. Today, through the video recorder even more powerful pornographic images are brought into the homes of our nation. And then what shall we say about the Internet, which has brought pornography shops into American homes? Many sit peering into the screen enjoying virtual images, in some instances translated live to the consumer. Recently a youth pastor in a Chicago suburb had to resign because of the reams of pornography he had downloaded from a Web site.

When we linked our computer to the World Wide Web, I had a dream that night of evil beings trying to pin me against a wall in my own home. It was a horrific experience, but I interpreted it as a warning from God. Something had entered our home that would seek to destroy me; Satan had a plan to ruin me right where I lived. I'm grateful for that warning, for if I am ever tempted to enter the dark world of Internet pornography, I just have to remember that I would be submitting to an enemy whose goal is my undoing.

Businessmen who stay in motels have the opportunity to see pornography, often without cost, in their rooms. Even if they don't order a movie, the cable channels are filled with every kind of pornography imaginable, along with violence and the occult. A writer for television sitcoms is quoted as saying, "We must get people to laugh at homosexuality, adultery and incest, because laughing breaks down their resistance to it."

Some therapists even tell their patients that they need to experience their "dark side" in order to be helped. They lead them into the world of pornography and sexual experience. That, of course, is equivalent to telling a mouse, "You have to try traps before you really are able to master them. Go find some cheese, feel the power of a trap, and you will awaken with new self-understanding."

The snare of pornography is different from most others in this book. Although we're all born greedy, we're not necessarily born with a love for gambling. We are not born with a love for alcohol but must acquire it by beginning to drink. But because we grow up with persistent sexual appetites, sexual fantasies are never far from our minds. Our sexuality is so much a part of who we are that it is almost impossible (especially for men) to live without battling impure thoughts. A hymn by George Heath expresses the danger.

> My soul, be on thy guard;
> Ten thousand foes arise;
> A host of sins are pressing hard
> To draw thee from the skies.

According to James Dobson, half of the Christian men surveyed struggle with pornography at some level. My suspicion is that in the non-Christian world, the users must approach 100 percent. With all the restraints gone, and with society having tolerated pornography in so many different ways, one must have a good reason to reject it. People no longer have to look for it. Pornography has come to them, and they must make an intentional choice to say no.

Charles Swindoll is right when he says that lust is no respecter of persons. "It never gives up; it never runs out of ideas. Bolt your front door, and it will rattle at the bedroom window, crawl into the living room through the TV screen, or wink at you out of a magazine in the den."[2] Those of us who have never been lured by gambling, alcoholism, or drugs can understand the lure of these addictions because we have found sexual temptation to be powerful and unrelenting. Some of us who have had the good fortune of escaping the snare of pornography have done so only because of external restraints and the inner grace granted by God. It is not difficult for me to see why pornography would hold such a powerful attraction to the average American male. And, yes, to females too. But if we want to "see God," purity of heart is necessary (Matthew 5:8).

Is pornography just a harmless pleasure?

## THE EFFECTS OF PORNOGRAPHY

You've probably heard the old line that pornography is a "victimless crime" and that it has no detrimental effects on users. That is a lie; just ask the wives of husbands immersed in pornography. Or, just have an honest conversation with a "user" and read the reports of sexual offenders.

First, we must keep in mind that there is a clear connection between pornography and other vices and even crimes. There is no doubt that when you see perversion, you want to act out perversion. A man who walked past an open window and became tantalized about raping a woman whose form he had seen did just that "to see what it was like." He later testified, as have many other rapists, that he was greatly influenced by the sexual violence he had seen in pornography.

Pornography makes men (and perhaps women too) seek some new thrill, some new way to express their inflamed desires. The fact that one out of every four girls born in the United States this year will at some time be molested is to a great degree the result of pornography, the exploitation of sexual desires. When Hugh Hefner began pornography in earnest, back in 1953, somebody's wife or daughter was not being raped every six minutes. Pedophilia was rare; now it happens every day every hour. Every form of perversion is available in pornography, and as those desires are acted out, the result is sex crimes of various sorts.

Yes, it is true that not everyone who is a user commits a crime. We've learned that not all who drink are alcoholics, not all gamblers are addicted, and as we shall see, not everyone who is connected to the occult is possessed by demons. Whereas an alcoholic harms primarily himself, a sex addict is looking for victims. Pornography is not a victimless crime.

Second, pornography, even if it does not lead to sex crimes, does lead millions into damaging sexual experiences. A young woman who had no lesbian desires became enamored with lesbian pornography on the Internet. She found herself intrigued by something that had previously repulsed her. Soon she found herself seeking out a lesbian partner to experience what she had seen. God only knows the number of people who have been led into perverted sexual experiences because of the lure of the material they have watched.

Keep in mind the basic principle given by Jesus: "I tell you the truth, everyone who sins is a slave to sin. Now a slave has no permanent place in the family, but a son belongs to it forever. So if the Son sets you free, you will be free indeed" (John 8:34–36). Slaves do not made decisions; they carry out the wishes of someone else. Slaves wake up in the morning and receive their orders for the day, obeying the commands of their master. Just so, when we are slaves to sin, our lives are out of our control. Any one of us could commit any form of sexual perversion if we just submitted ourselves to it on the Internet, videos, or cable television. The images of pornography enslave their worshipers.

A woman who was awakened in the middle of the night heard her husband talking on the telephone. To her surprise and chagrin, he was surrounded by pornographic magazines and having phone sex. Turns out that he had racked up hundreds of dollars of telephone bills on credit cards as he dutifully satisfied his desires. How did this addiction come about? Very simply. He picked up the phone one day and called the "toll-free" number that had been advertised on television. Consistent with the words of Jesus, he became a slave to the sin to which he submitted himself. A single phone call was the beginning of this man's dark, secret journey to sexual enslavement.

Not everyone is like the man I met in Washington, D.C., who spends $400 a month on pornography. Not everyone is like the missionary who returned home and bought a thousand dollars worth of porno videos. There are many "casual" users who might not spend any money on pornography as such but take advantage of what can be seen in drug stores, on the Internet, and on TV.

Third, pornography is harmful because of what it does to relationships. This goddess will always cry "more," and her needs will never be satisfied. The obsession is self-perpetuating, and therefore openness and honesty in a relationship (particularly marriage) is marred. Men become dissatisfied with their wives; the woman's self-esteem is destroyed because she knows she can never measure up to the images of the beautiful models. Men often ask their wives to participate in repulsive acts because of what they have seen in pornography.

For the users there is an obsession with the forbidden, and since pornography is usually viewed in private, there is a cloud of guilt and the motivation to live a double life.

Finally, pornography affects the soul, the mind, the emotions, and the will. A woman who discovered that her husband was using pornography and abusing her children wrote, "Pornography is built on a world of fantasy; you create your own consequences. In the real world you do A, and B happens. But in pornography, you do A, and you can create your own B."[3] She went on to explain how this fantasy defiles the deepest part of the soul. The effects of shame and the desire to re-create titillating experiences lead to helpless submission to whatever impulses come to the human heart. Yes, pornography kills the soul and steals the heart. Worse, it grieves God.

Where do we turn for help? What hope is there for the person who told me that even when he participates in singing hymns at church the images he saw that week flood his mind? What do we say to the person who asks forgiveness, only to indulge again? What do we do with the observation from the book of Proverbs, "Death and Destruction are never satisfied, and neither are the eyes of man" (Proverbs 27:20)?

## WARNINGS FROM THE WORD

The struggle for purity of mind and heart did not begin with the invention of the cinema. The apostle Peter, writing to believers who lived in an immoral culture, wrote, "Dear friends, I urge you, as aliens and strangers in the world, to abstain from sinful desires, which war against your soul. Live such good lives among the pagans that, though they accuse you of doing wrong, they may see your good deeds and glorify God on the day he visits us" (1 Peter 2:11–12). In the same book, Peter tells believers that they should be done with sin, living lives not for evil human desires but rather for the will of God. He commends them to be free of "debauchery, lust, drunkenness, orgies, carousing and detestable idolatry" (4:3). Yes, we must live free from the debasing practices of the world.

First, Peter says, we should "abstain from sinful desires" because we are *different* from the world. We are "aliens" and "strangers" who should not adopt the customs of the country in which we live. We don't participate in the customs of the locals, who know the details of the cultural terrain. Just so, we have no reason to explore all of the exotic offerings of this world, for we know that we are on our way to another world, a *holy* world.

We travel light, knowing that we are just passing through to a better land. We are at best "ignorant" of evil, not satisfying our curiosity with all of the possibilities sensuality has to offer. Just like an alcoholic for whom one drink might send him on a binge, so one immersion in the world of pornography might begin a secret lifestyle of satisfying inflamed cravings.

Second, Peter says, we are also at *war* with the world. These lusts wage "war against your soul." Lust aims to win, to control, to dominate, to take possession. Yet, there is the part of us that does not want to surrender such control. We want God to be first in our lives, but lust does not listen to our reasonable pleas. Temptation comes with the express desire of overwhelming us; we are at war whether we like it or not. If we declare a truce, the Enemy will take advantage of our weakness. At stake is the health of our soul.

I've heard even Christians say that the biblical standard is far too high; we simply have to make allowance for the stimuli we cannot avoid. "Better to control the input as best we can, rather than try to end it altogether," it is said. What is more, lust is pleasurable, and to be too victorious would cut us off from enjoyable experiences. Maybe being an "occasional user" will not disrupt our fellowship with God.

Yes, it is true that we cannot entirely avoid the enticing images that come to us from television, newspapers, billboards, and the like. Temptation, we have learned, seeks us out; but we must avoid putting ourselves in temptation's path. This is a fight to the finish, for lust comes to us with the oft-quoted dictum "What is mine is mine and what is yours is negotiable." Thus the battle continues.

Finally, Peter says, we are *observed* by the world. Concerning waging a successful war against lust, he writes, "Live such good lives among the pagans that, though they accuse you of doing wrong, they may see your good deeds and glorify God on the day he visits us" (1 Peter 2:12). If we become a part of the moral pollution around us, we have compromised our message with the world. There is a direct connection between the purity of our lives and the power of our witness to the world. It is difficult for us to stand up in the world when we are full of rot on the inside.

Take a moment to think of the people you know who have lost their witness to the world because they have fallen into sexual sin. I'm not just thinking of the highly publicized sins of the televangelists of the 1980s, but of ministers and missionaries, of Bible teachers and otherwise devoted husbands and fathers. A minister who often spoke in various churches spent most of his secret moments poring over the latest pornographic magazine. When he was finally able to talk about his struggle and seek help, he made this observation: "I could rationalize what I was doing, except for one fact: I knew that what I was doing grieved the Lord I loved and my habit disrupted my fellowship with Him, and that hurt." Yes, a life of impurity, even if shielded from human eyes, grieves God.

Drastic action is needed.

## THE TOUGH LOVE OF JESUS

If we think Jesus is going to let us make excuses for our lusts, we are sorely mistaken. Perhaps no passage in all the Bible speaks so directly to the issue of lust and pornography as the words from the lips of the Master Himself: "You have heard that it was said, 'Do not commit adultery.' But I tell you that anyone who looks at a woman lustfully has already committed adultery with her in his heart" (Matthew 5:27–28).

He knew that all men would be indicted by this standard! He anticipated our incredulous response and went on to explain that parting with lust is almost like parting with a member of the body. So he added, "If your right eye causes you to sin, gouge it out and throw it away. It is better for you to lose one part of your body than for your whole body to be thrown into hell. And if your right hand causes you to sin, cut it off and throw it away. It is better for you to lose one part of your body than for your whole body to go into hell" (Matthew 5:29–30).

The phrase "causes you to sin" refers to a stumbling block. According to Barclay, it means "bait stick in a trap."[4] The picture is that of a pit dug into the ground and deceptively covered with a thin layer of branches so that the unwary animal will "fall into the pit." Christ is saying that if your eye or hand causes you to trip up, *if you find yourself submitting to the power of lust, take drastic action!*

Jesus began with the eye, since that is how lust, particularly for men, begins. We've already spoken of the exotic stimulation of pictures, whether on the big screen, television, or a computer monitor. Indeed, pornography takes advantage of every angle, form, and shade of lighting to ignite the most powerful response.

Then, Jesus spoke of the hand, which represents a further stage in sexual arousal, particularly for women. Tender words coupled with tender caresses often lead to sexual stimulation and involvement. He now says that if the eye must be cut out or the hand cut off, so be it. For "it is better for you to lose one part of your body than for your whole body to go into hell."

Needless to say, Christ was speaking figuratively. To submit to some form of mutilation to deaden the passions of lust is hardly what He had in mind. Even if a man cut out his right eye, he could still lust with his left one! And to get rid of the hand would hardly curb the sexual desires of the body. No, this is not literal.

But, in this sense, Christ's words are quite literally true; it would be better to lose an eye in this life than to enter hell with two! And it would be better to have one hand (if such were possible) in heaven rather than enter hell with two! What Christ is saying in the strongest possible way is this: Be willing to do whatever is necessary to keep from falling into the "pit."

Jesus knew that our hands and eyes are highly prized; we'd do anything to spare them. We wouldn't part with them unless absolutely necessary. Lust is as difficult to part with as a hand or an eye. Anyone who knows the exhilaration of sexual attraction knows that. And yet He says we must make that choice, even at great personal cost.

## Amputation Is Painful

Sitting here in my study, I'm trying to visualize what amputation would be like! Imagine having one's eyes gouged out, or a hand cut off. In ancient times there was no anesthetic, no way to alleviate the throbbing torment that would accompany such an experience. No needles, drugs, or delicate surgical instruments—just crude cutting tools. Grotesque scars would remain as reminders of the ordeal.

Recently I spoke to a man who was in love with a woman who was not his wife. I explained that this relationship had to end; he had to return to his wife and rebuild his deteriorating marriage. He still had deep affection toward this other woman, along with feelings of "oneness" he had never known for his wife. I explained that he would have to end his "affair," even grieving over the loss. Jesus would say, "Even though it hurts, do it."

How do we take drastic action?

First, we must flee from the temptation. Paul's advice is "Flee from sexual immorality" (1 Corinthians 6:18). And again, "Flee the evil desires of youth" (2 Timothy 2:22). Run from temptation without leaving a forwarding address. When we find ourselves looking for stimuli, we are already on the path to defeat.

What if temptation is close—next door or on the job? The seed of sensuality must be crushed before it grows into a deeply rooted tree that will not budge. Eliminate visits to newsstands that carry pornography; take that Blockbuster card and cut it to bits. Phone your cable company and tell them you will discontinue their service.

Too drastic? That's not as drastic as gouging out your eye or cutting off your hand! Because we are not willing to take radical measures, our battle for purity is stalled. If we don't know what to do, let us pray, "Lead us not into temptation, but deliver us from evil." We must, in all sincerity, turn to God in submission and desperation. Whatever form our temptation takes, we must stop it, for it is sin sweetly poisoned.

Yes, it is painful. A young man told me that just throwing his pornographic pictures away that he had kept stashed in his garage was difficult. His habit had become so much a part of his life. But again, Christ would say, "No matter how painful—do it!"

## Amputation Is Thorough

Suppose you go to the doctor with a cancerous growth and he says, "I plan to do this in stages; I'll cut out most of it this time and take more later. We won't decide now whether we will take it all."

Absurd? Of course. You want him to cut a trifle beyond the growth to make sure that he "got it all." And once the knife has cut the growth, there is no turning back. We can't rethink it and say, "I wonder if I should have done this."

Benjamin Needler, a Puritan writer, put it this way: "We must not part with sin, as with a friend, with a purpose to see it again and to have the same familiarity as before, or possibly greater. . . . We must shake our hands of it as Paul did shake the viper off his hand into the fire."[5] Yes, we must burn every bridge behind us—no turning back (remember Lot's wife?). Just as the ancient Jews searched their houses with a candle to be sure there was no leaven left among them, we must with the same diligence search our lives lest there be poison that is defiling our whole body. With God's help and intervention, sin must be pulled out though it resists like a tooth in the jaw. Paul reminded us to "clothe [ourselves] with the Lord Jesus Christ, and . . . not think about how to gratify the desires of the sinful nature" (Romans 13:14).

A. W. Tozer was right when he said, "That part of us that we rescue from the cross may be a very little part of us, but it is likely to be the seat of our spiritual troubles and our defeats." Our tendency to "make provision for the flesh" by refusing to close all the doors to temptation opens us up for the devil's continued assault.

If there is one single reason why many are unable to break the power of sexual sin (such as pornography), it can be simply stated: they have not made a radical commitment to holiness in every area of their lives. God is consulted for forgiveness and emotional healing, but often he is not invited to uproot the sin through complete across-the-board submission.

Somewhere I read that when you are going to jump across a chasm it is much better to do it in one long jump than in two short ones! Just so, when we deal with sin in our lives, it is best that it be done thoroughly, completely, and without making it easy to retrace our steps. Again, Jesus would say, "Do it."

## Amputation Is Worthwhile

Is the pain worth it? Just ask the cancer patient who has been told by the doctor, "We got it all." The soul is worth more than the hand or the eye; just so, the joy of freedom is better than the slavery of impurity. Christian Bovee said, "The body of a sensualist is the coffin of the dead soul."

Let's take a moment to contemplate that man who has but one eye and one hand. Obviously, he is not able to fulfill his cherished dreams. Since the hopes of a lifetime are shattered, the best he can do is adjust to a host of unfulfilled desires. He'll have to bury his plans and resurrect more simple goals. He must either adjust or self-destruct. Yet, Christ would say, "It is better . . ."

Better to live with a disability than to live in defiance of God; better to face life with an unfulfilled marriage as a friend of God than to incur God's displeasure. God is a friend to the lonely, to those with unfulfilled dreams or desires, but He will judge those who commit immorality. "Marriage should be honored by all, and the marriage bed kept pure, for God will judge the adulterer and all the sexually immoral" (Hebrews 13:4). If the choice is between losing an eye or losing our soul, let us have our eye cut out; if the choice is between losing a hand or losing our soul, let us have our hand cut off.

Jesus knows our disappointments. Jesus would agree that it is better to remain single and frustrated (though I don't mean to imply that all singles are frustrated) than to have a relationship that breaks God's command. There is something worse than loneliness and lack of fulfillment, and that is to displease the Lord.

As Walter Trobisch put it, "The task we have to face is the same, whether we are married or single: to live a fulfilled life in spite of many unfulfilled desires."[6] Sexual sin, no matter how appealing, is never worth more than an arm or a leg. Someone has said, "How prompt we are to satisfy the hunger and thirst of our bodies; how slow to satisfy the hunger and thirst of our souls."

## COMING TO THE LIGHT

"If I ever catch you with a magazine like this again, I'm out of here. What are you, some kind of a pervert!?" Those were the words of a wife to a husband when she discovered the magazine hidden in the closet. Just think of what this woman did: first, she took his habit as a personal attack against her (which in one sense it was, but in another sense it was not); and second, she only added to her husband's shame. If we remember that shame fuels addiction, she had just given him one more reason to sink into the dark world of pornography. He already believed he was scum, and now the most significant person in his life had just confirmed it.

Understandably, pornography is repulsive to most women, but think of how much more helpful it would had been if she had said, "What you have done hurts me, but I love you; I know you have fallen into a snare, but I want to be here to help you. I promise to encourage you and to love you. Let's face all of this together."

This approach would have had two benefits. His secret would be out in the open, which would have been of great help in restoration and healing. Many men find that when their hidden sin is exposed to someone who still sees them as worthy of love, there is a great emotional release. At last, the charade is over, the guilt and shame of leading a secret life has come to an end. This is the day they have dreaded, but now that it is here they can be thankful that the time for healing has come. When a man's desire for deliverance is greater than his desire to hide his shame, help is on the way.

Also, if this man's wife had spoken to him in an understanding way, he would have been given the assurance that though he had failed, his marriage and future were worth salvaging. Many men who struggle with pornography do love their wives, but the seductive images to which they have given themselves are powerful and unrelenting. My advice to wives: stand alongside your husband with a spirit of helpfulness, prayer, and encouragement. If not, he will be driven back into his world of sexual obsession veiled in an even more secretive shroud.

I agree with those counselors who tell us that it is not possible for an addict to come clean until he has come into the light; that is, until his secret is shared. Satan works undercover; his kingdom is one of darkness and shame. When the lid is lifted and the light of truth shines into the soul, there is hope and cleansing. Men who cannot share their struggle with their wives must confide in a friend, counselor, or pastor with whom they can pray and be accountable. If Jesus, the perfect Son of God, asked that three of His disciples pray with Him in the dark battle of Gethsemane, it should not be difficult for us to confess that we need the help of others in our own battle against sin.

Second, along with this sharing must come accountability. As in other addictions, those who are caught in the web of pornography will always have a tendency to revert back to their addiction of choice. Only after death will temptation no longer stalk us. God uses our struggles to humble us, to show us the great need we have for one another. You may have fallen into the pit on your own, but you will need others to help you out.

Third, God's forgiveness must be accepted. The cleansing of the conscience is very important in our battle for purity. Guilt and unresolved issues that lie within the soul will always agitate for expression and resolution. If we do not find our peace in the presence of Jesus, we will seek to find pleasure to divert the pain. When Jesus was confronted with a woman taken in adultery, He said to her accusers, "If any one of you is without sin, let him be the first to throw a stone at her." Those who heard his words walked out, one at a time. When no one remained to condemn her, He replied, "Neither do I condemn you. . . . Go now and leave your life of sin" (John 8:7, 11).

Thankfully, moral impurity, of whatever kind, is not an unforgivable sin. Jesus died for sinners; our failures disappoint Him, but they do not surprise Him. We can affirm, "If we confess our sins, he is faithful and just and will forgive us our sins and purify us from all unrighteousness" (1 John 1:9). We can not only be forgiven but made pure; our conscience can be cleansed. In the presence of Jesus there is forgiveness and hope.

As for the consequences of our sin, we must leave these with God. We cannot control what has happened because of our disobedience; we can, however, acknowledge that the God who forgives us is the God who brings healing and restoration. As long as we are alive He has some purpose for us and our work is not yet finished.

Finally, as in any temptation, our minds are strengthened when they are renewed. Jesus said that when an evil spirit comes out of a man, it wanders seeking rest.

> *"Then it says, 'I will return to the house I left.' When it arrives, it finds the house unoccupied, swept clean and put in order. Then it goes and takes with it seven other spirits*

*more wicked than itself, and they go in and live there.*
*And the final condition of that man is worse than the first."*

—MATTHEW 12:44–45

The Lord's point is that Satan will take any part of our souls that is unoccupied; he will take advantage of our emptiness, our lack of preparation for his assaults. Pornography is the devil's territory, and he does not play by the rules. When we spend time in his domain, we are in for a fight to reclaim the rights of our God-given inheritance. But claim them we must.

How do we win the battle with impure thoughts? Here is an experiment: Try to stop thinking about the number seven! Try as we might, it is not possible to get that number out of our mind, once it is there. But we can substitute other thoughts: for example, if we focus our mind on our father or mother, we will soon forget about the number seven. Just so, we must fill our minds with Scripture so that we can resist Satan's attacks.

One day a young man came to ask how he could stop browsing porno magazines at a newsstand. He loved God; he was in Christian service and effective. I asked him to make a promise that before he picked up one of those magazines, he had to recite five verses of Scripture and go through them about three or four times before making up his mind as to what he would do.

Here are sample verses:

- "Blessed are the pure in heart, for they will see God" (Matthew 5:8).
- "Do not conform any longer to the pattern of this world, but be transformed by the renewing of your mind. Then you will be able to test and approve what God's will is—his good, pleasing and perfect will" (Romans 12:2).
- "But we have the mind of Christ" (1 Corinthians 2:16b).
- "But among you there must not be even a hint of sexual immorality, or of any kind of impurity, or of greed, because these are improper for God's holy people. . . . For of this you can be sure: No immoral, impure or greedy person—such a man is an

idolater—has any inheritance in the kingdom of Christ and of God" (Ephesians 5:3, 5).

• "Finally, brothers, whatever is true, whatever is noble, whatever is right, whatever is pure, whatever is lovely, whatever is admirable—if anything is excellent or praiseworthy—think about such things" (Philippians 4:8).

Soon after he had readied his "battle plan," God sent a trial his way. A misplaced pornographic magazine arrived in his apartment mailbox. As he held it in his hands, he remembered the promise he had made: he would have to recite all the verses at least three times before he opened the pages. We can imagine him there in the apartment saying, "Blessed are the pure in heart for they shall see God . . ." When he was finished quoting the Scripture, he was able to throw the magazine away without opening it. That was the first in a series of victories.

At all costs we cannot give up the fight. No matter how often we lose, the battle must be enjoined. We fight with this assurance: "In this world you will have trouble. But take heart! I have overcome the world" (John 16:33b).

## A PRAYER TO BEGIN THE JOURNEY

*Father, I confess that pornography is sin. I admit that I have willingly believed Satan's lie that since the human body is beautiful, I have a right to gaze upon it to fulfill my lusts. I acknowledge that Your Word commands me to be holy and blameless, and that the lusts of the flesh are of the world. Forgive me for grieving the Spirit through my rationalizations and unbelief.*

*I now take back all the ground I have given to Satan by watching sensual images on television, the Internet, and videos. I break this stronghold of the Enemy in the powerful name of Jesus. In faith, I accept my one-*

ness with Christ and I choose to not "let sin reign in [my] mortal body so that [I] obey its evil desires" (Romans 6:12).

Let me be willing to pay the price of humility and accountability in breaking my secret habit. I affirm today that I am accountable to Christ and acknowledge Him as Lord of my mind, my heart, and my body. I commit to a life of holiness, whatever the cost.

In Jesus' name, Amen.

# THE SEXUAL AFFAIR: A POISONED OASIS

*D*espite my determination to be faithful to my wife," the letter began, "the love had drained out of our marriage. Then I met this woman at work and we talked for hours about everything—our childhood, our marriages, our likes and dislikes. We ended up having an affair not because of sex, but because we both believed we had met our 'soul mate.' You'll never know the exhilaration of being with someone whom you actually love and can't be without."

The rest of the letter was quite predictable. When he first married, he believed marriage was for keeps, but when he and his wife began to have "irreconcilable differences" and he met the one for whom his soul longed, he woke up one morning and asked himself, "Is this the way I want to live for the next twenty years?" Having answered no to that question, he concluded that despite the emotional cost to his wife and children, despite his Christian testimony, despite what the Bible said, the only reasonable thing to do was marry the woman with whom he had experienced true intimacy. He might have quoted the words of Woody Allen, "The heart wants what it wants."

It's been many years since this man left his wife to marry the woman of his dreams. When we tried to convince him to break off his adulterous relationship, he told us, "I have lived in a desert for so many years; now I have found an oasis, but you insist that I go back to the desert." So he left the desert and opted for the "oasis" that gave him the nurture he wanted. Here at last he found someone who listened; someone who understood, that "soul mate" with whom he could be one in body and spirit.

But eleven years later he wrote me a letter confessing that his oasis had become so bitter that he wished he had stayed in the desert! He learned that there are some things worse than sexual loneliness; one is sexual "fulfillment" outside of the will and purpose of God. Better to die in the desert pleasing the Lord than drink poison from the devil's cisterns.

There is a legend about a girl walking through the woods who almost stepped on a snake. Instinctively, she pulled back in horror, but to her amazement, the snake called out, "I'm so glad you came along. I'm cold and need a friend. Please pick me up and put me under you coat so that I can get warm, and will you be my friend?"

In fear, the girl replied, "I cannot possibly do that. You're a rattlesnake and you will bite me. I *can't* pick you up."

"No, I promise I won't bite you. I really want to be your friend, and after all, am I not also a creature of God, just like you? I'm so cold; please pick me up."

She began to feel sorry for the snake and sat down to think it over. As she looked at this creature of God, it began to look beautiful; previously she had not noticed its many colors. She admired its graceful lines and movement, and gradually it began to look harmless.

She thought, *Well, he's right. He is a creature of God. And just because most rattlesnakes bite doesn't mean this one will. It seems like a nice snake, and shouldn't I be willing to be a friend when someone asks me? Someone who needs me?*

"Yes, I'll be your friend," she said, and picked up the snake and put it under her warm coat.

Immediately, the snake bit her, and the pain and poison shot through her body. She cried out, "Why did you bite me . . . You *promised* you would be my friend!"

The rattlesnake wiggled away, turned with a smirk, and said, *"You knew what I was when you picked me up!"*

Yes, we know sexual sin is a rattlesnake. But how desperately we convince ourselves that *this* time, with *this* person, in *this* context, for *these* reasons, it will not bite!

We live in a world of sexual freedom. A world of pornography (as we learned in the last chapter) and a world in which people are seeking meaningful relationships. Some seek intimacy just to fulfill their desires; others do so because they have found someone with whom they can have a rewarding relationship—or so it seems. But out from under the protection of marriage and cut loose from a God-sanctioned love relationship, the cost of these relationships is too high.

Satan is sly with us. He knows that as Christians we have good taste and good motives. He does not tempt us with cheap things or brazen sin, because those would not appeal to our spiritual nature. Rather, he subtly takes some very good gift of God, such as intimacy and oneness of spirit, and interjects into that gift some qualities that are not pleasing to God. He distorts our priorities and tempts us to use God's good things in the wrong place or time. Thus sexual attraction may become a problem in a perfectly proper love relationship.[1]

Anyone looking for an affair of any kind can find one. Our problem is that sexual relationships can be developed without our searching for them. The office, the backyard, the church, or the hotel lobby: in all of these places we can meet vulnerable people who are looking for meaningful intimate relationships. And increasingly we hear of "online affairs" developed in Internet chat rooms. Anyone can commit sexual sin: committed Christians, uncommitted Christians, doctors, lawyers, truck drivers, and ministers. We all are tempted.

Sometimes we think that immorality exists primarily among the young people who say they cannot wait until marriage. Not true; the formerly married struggle greatly with their sexual relationships. Millions of people are either divorced or have lost a mate through death. Since you cannot turn sexual desires off like a water faucet, the desire to "reconnect" with someone is ever present. Surveys show that many formerly married adults are not celibate. Understandably, they struggle with the conflict of their faith and experience. Comments like this are often heard:

"Sometimes I feel so despondent after having been out—having a good time in companionship and sexuality—that I feel as if I want to die rather than live this torn-apart feeling."

"I felt the need to prove my sexuality to myself and to other men. . . . But that inner conflict between my sexual needs and moral and spiritual needs still tears away at me. One part of me says, 'It is right and beautiful,' and the other part tells me, 'This is wrong as a Christian.'"

"I've prayed about my sexual needs and God has answered them and given me someone to relate with. I couldn't have planned it that way. Christ wants us to live abundant lives, and that includes sex."

"I feel guilt at myself for giving in and I have resentment toward the man who continues to push me."

Many of these people live in committed but unmarried relationships. Others have no hesitancy to move from one partner to another. Either way, there is no way to circumvent the displeasure of God with sin. "Marriage should be honored by all, and the marriage bed kept pure, for God will judge the adulterer and all the sexually immoral" (Hebrews 13:4).

If we break the commandments, they will break us. Pascal said, "Happiness is neither out of us or in us. It is in God." We can never find happiness at the expense of character; we cannot find happiness by stepping out of the boundaries God has prescribed for us. If only we were as committed to holiness as we are to happiness!

I'm told that in Switzerland there is an animal called the ermine who takes pride in his clean white fur. Hunters take cruel advantage of this trait and pour oil around the hole where the animal lives. When the ermine is hunted, it refuses to enter its own home for fear of getting its fur grimy. The ermine would rather die than have its coat besmudged. If only we had the same commitment to the purity of our souls as this animal has to the purity of its fur coat!

In the last chapter we discussed the snare of pornography, the stimulation of the mind with erotic images. This chapter takes us a step further, hoping to help those who act out their fantasies in some form of sexual expression. In a word, we are talking about common snares such as fornication, adultery, voyeurism, exhibitionism, and even child molestation, or the like. We all know people who are driven by some form of sexual compulsion, and most assuredly we all have been tempted.

Any one of us could be ensnared in one of the many traps of sexual immorality. As one man said, "This is where your game is played. Everything else is warm-ups and practice. The real game is played on this field and on this field only."[2] Millions who have said, "I never would," have had to ruefully admit, "I did."

Yes, sexual sin promises like a god but pays like the devil. It is upon this rock that lives are ruined, families are destroyed, and the testimony of the church is desecrated. The devil, in cahoots with perverted human nature, has manufactured lies about ourselves and our sexuality. And, oh, how quick we are to believe those lies. We *want* to believe them!

Today I invite you to come on a guided tour of the biblical understanding of sexuality. Our purpose is threefold.

First, to understand ourselves so that we might know how God created us and why fulfilling our sexual desires outside of prescribed limits is probably our greatest temptation. Here we understand our vulnerabilities.

Second, to finally understand the origins of that dark world of illicit sexuality, the world of addictions and obsessions. We will discover that sexual acts outside of marriage are definitely a desert, not an oasis; its waters are as bitter as those of Marah could ever be.

Third, to point the way out of the shadows into the light of sexual sanity and submission to God's will. Yes, thanks to His grace, there is hope for all.

Be patient as we embark on the journey.

## SEXUALITY AND CREATION

Think of it: though Adam had the awesome privilege of walking with God in the garden, God said something important was missing! "It is not good for the man to be alone. I will make a helper suitable for him" (Genesis 2:18). God clearly affirms that man is a social creature and needs companionship that is "suitable" for him.

When God created Adam, He chose to use the dust of the ground for the raw material. "The LORD God formed the man from the dust of the ground and breathed into his nostrils the breath of life, and the man became a living being" (Genesis 2:7).

We might expect God would make a similar form from dust when He created Eve. But we read, "So the Lord God caused the man to fall into a deep sleep; and while he was sleeping, he took one of the man's ribs and closed up the place with flesh. Then the LORD God made a woman from the rib he had taken out of the man, and he brought her to the man" (Genesis 2:21–22).

God separated femininity out of masculinity, forming two separate people created in His image. With this separation came a powerful implanted desire in the male and the female to be reunited in an intimate oneness. Sexuality would be fundamental to personhood; whether male or female, our sexual identity occupies our thoughts and shapes our self-image.

God gave Adam and Eve different characteristics. Men tend to be aggressive and depend upon a rational analysis of life's problems. Women have a strong sense of intuition, basic trust, and sensitivity. Obviously, these are generalizations, and there is overlapping. The point is simply that both genders mirror different aspects of the image of God. Though they both have the image of God, they reflect God in different ways.

In marriage, these characteristics are united in a harmony that should enhance man's representation of God. Paul taught that marriages should give a visual display of the relationship between Christ and the church.

Here in the Creation account are the roots of our sexual natures, proof that sex was created by God as an expression of unity and love between a man and a woman. Two implications follow: (1) We must accept our sexual desires as from God, and (2) we should positively affirm our sexuality. The innate attraction between a man and a woman is powerful and unyielding. If Adam had not been sexually attracted to Eve, the human race would have ended with the death of our two parents. But God made the desire for physical intimacy so strong there was no chance that Adam would look at Eve and walk away!

Marriage reflects the plurality and unity of the Godhead. Though God exists in three persons, we read, "Hear, O Israel: The LORD our

God, the LORD is one" (Deuteronomy 6:4). The same Hebrew word for one (*ehad*) is used for the marriage union: "And they will become one flesh" (Genesis 2:24). Just as it is unthinkable that the members of the Trinity would operate as separate entities, so a husband and wife should live together with both diversity and unity. The bond that has been formed involves the total personality of each partner.

In summary, sex creates a "soul tie" between two people, forming the most intimate of all human relationships. We read that "Adam knew Eve his wife" (Genesis 4:1 KJV). When they made love together, they experienced the highest form of interpersonal communication and knowledge. Once a man and woman have been sexually intimate, nothing can ever be quite the same between them again. There is no such thing as a brand new beginning.

God intended that the first sexual experience be enjoyed by a man and woman committed to each other and bound together by a covenant. Complete acceptance and unconditional love were to be guarded by a lifelong commitment. Once that commitment is compromised, the partners are diminished; worse, a series of consequences follows that has far-reaching implications.

Keep reading.

## SEXUALITY AND ALIEN BONDS

What happens when an individual is sexually active outside of the male-female covenant in marriage?

Such relationships create what can be called an "alien bond," that is, an illicit bond with another human being. In all such relationships, whether male and female, lesbian or homosexual, a metaphysical bond is developed between the participants. Both personalities have been intimately united with each other with consequences for future relationships with other partners. And, in a moment, I will explain why and how those illicit "soul ties" often lead to a life of addiction.

Perhaps one of the most instructive passages in the New Testament that helps us understand our sexuality is found in Paul's words to the Corinthian church:

*Do you not know that your bodies are members of Christ himself? Shall I then take the members of Christ and unite them with a prostitute? Never! Do you not know that he who unites himself with a prostitute is one with her in body? For it is said, "The two will become one flesh." But he who unites himself with the Lord is one with him in spirit.*

—1 CORINTHIANS 6:15-16

Follow this carefully. We all agree that sex with a prostitute is sex without a commitment, sex without any hint of mutual respect or caring. Prostitution is based on raw lust, sex for money, sex for mutual exploitation. Yet, incredibly, Paul says that God joins the prostitute to her partner and "the two will become one flesh." To prove it, he quotes Genesis 2:24, where God joins Adam and Eve, making them one flesh. *Sex of any kind—even immoral sexual experiences— bind the participants together, body, soul, and spirit.*

A woman whose husband asked forgiveness for his promiscuity said, "I feel as if all the other women he has had sex with are in bed there with me." She is right in two ways. First, AIDS researchers tell us that when we have a sexual relationship, we are, in effect, having sex with all the other people our partner has had sex with. But this is also true in a second sense, namely, that the promiscuous partner has been joined metaphysically to each of his or her partners. God has made them "one" with each other.

What are some of the consequences of these "alien" bonds? What happens when we decide to step outside of God's boundaries? Why, for example does sexually molesting a child mean that he or she might develop sexual compulsions or struggle with gender identity?

## The Power of the First Bond

Sex outside of marriage has far-reaching consequences because of the "bonds" that are created through the experience. A boy recruited by an older male homosexual may initially hate the experience, but because sex unites two people, he might begin to feel a sense of security and fulfillment within this relationship. Soon he seeks out other male partners, not because he was born a homosexual, but because his initial experiences are so stamped on his soul. As he grows up he follows the lead of his newly awakened desires.

This also explains why a young woman may marry a man with whom she has slept even though he is abusive. His personality is indelibly imprinted on her mind and heart; she feels this bond, this obligation to become his wife. Because of this sinful bond, he may have a great deal of power over her. He may mistreat her, but she returns to him. Even if the relationship ends, it will be difficult for her to put him out of her mind.

Given the importance of the first sexual experiences, even older people will be tempted to return to a previous (usually the first) sexual partner. Read this letter that arrived in my mailbox:

> I am in great need of help to bring closure to a relationship that ended years ago. I have since married someone else, yet have felt no relief from thinking about the other man. This inner conflict has caused great problems for our marriage. It seems as if I am in limbo, unable to fully let go of the past relationship and unable to fully love my husband. I did all that I could to separate myself from my first lover, including transferring to another college; that was five years ago. Meanwhile, I married a wonderful Christian man, but I am sick of thinking about my past lover. I fear that, in trying to gain relief from this anxiety, I will do something to ultimately harm my marriage.

This woman had sexually bonded with her lover, but though she left the relationship and married another man, she cannot get the previous man out of her mind and heart. If they had only dated without having sex, there is no doubt that she would find it much easier to love her present husband and not focus on a past relationship. But the first sexual bonds are often particularly powerful and long lasting.

Think of the implications for a child molested by an adult! The sexual identity of the child might be confused because the boundaries of protection have been violated. This opens the child up to a possible lifestyle of sexual dysfunction. Recently, I spoke to a woman who was sexually abused by her father. To this day she still has difficulty staying within proper boundaries, even as a wife and mother. She is still looking for the love of a father, but of course cannot find it. With her sexual confusion and pain it is difficult for her to remain true to her marriage covenant.

Some 80 percent of all lesbians were molested by a man, often a father, a baby-sitter, a relative, or a stranger. As these girls grow up, they are angry with men, so find it more convenient to stay with those who are of their own gender. Lesbianism for women, like homosexuality for men, is a shortcut to intimacy. It is having a sexual relationship without having to navigate the difficult problem of relating to the opposite sex.

Yes, there may be instances where confusion of gender cannot be traced to sexual abuse, pornography, or a dysfunctional family. But our sexuality is sacred, and whenever the boundaries are violated the consequences are as deep as the soul.

## A Tendency to Promiscuity

Once an illicit sexual bond is formed, there will be a desire to maintain that bond or seek other ones to replace it. A young woman told me she entered the world of illicit relationships at the age of twenty-six. She was tired of virginity and decided it was her turn to enjoy the sexual relationship. When it ended (as it always does), she thought she almost heard the words, "Now that you are defiled . . . you might as well do it again." This began a whole spiral of sexual relationships, always looking for that "perfect" person, that perfectly fulfilling union.

A man who visited a prostitute "just once" found himself unable to stop his moral slide. When he was discovered, he admitted that he had been seeing a prostitute twice a week despite the fact that he was married and had a child. I cannot count the number of singles whose stories I have listened to who have chosen to live together, broken up, and then have gone from one partner to another, ever seeking the fulfillment they desire. Some appear helpless to resist any sexual opportunity.

One addict tells of his unrelenting sexual desires: "I looked at every woman to lust, wondering if I could seduce her. For every one I seduced, there were ten I wanted to have, but could not." Thus the vicious cycle of sexuality keeps spiraling out of control.

Many people deny that guilt must accompany illicit sexual relationships, but of necessity there is shame and guilt. God did not create us for alien bonds, and such relationships violate His will. Because sexuality is such a sensitive part of who we are as persons, a residue of guilt will surface in those relationships. Those who deny guilt actually have only learned how to "manage" it.

## TOURING AN ADDICT'S WORLD

Perhaps now we are in a better position to understand why the life of a sex addict is usually traceable to one or more sexual experiences that began the long spiraling journey into the world of sexual oblivion. Usually it was that first act where the consequences seemed manageable. "I'll just do this once to satisfy my curiosity," or, "I know what I'm doing and will accept the consequences." Whatever, the "alien bond" awakens desires that plunge the participant into a fierce battle of sexual temptation—a battle so intense the victim sees little reason to fight, since it appears to be a lost cause.

Since sexual addictions grow best in the soil of ruptured relationships, we should not be surprised that Michael Castleman writes, "Sex addicts use sex like a drug, not to consummate loving relationships but rather to drown the pain of feeling empty inside a dark, shameful well of sexual oblivion."[3] Yet, of course, the relationships only increase the emptiness. As the survey respondent quoted earlier said, "Sometimes I feel so despondent after having been out—having a good time in companionship and sexuality—that I feel as if I want to die rather than live this 'torn apart' feeling."

Those who pursue a lifestyle of sexual pleasure usually resolve to live differently moments after another failure when their psyche is awash with feelings of regret and shame. But within time they will rationalize their behavior. The man who visits prostitutes will say, "I really do still love my wife," or, "It can't be so bad because so many people do it." The exhibitionist will gloat in his ability to remain undetected, telling himself that his euphoric pleasure does not hinder his interpersonal relationships. Thoughts about God are pushed out of the mind with the vague belief that such matters will be taken up in due time. In the depths of his soul he knows he is being untrue to himself, to others, and to God. So he will try to manage his guilt on an intellectual level, making up all manner of lies that he is eager to believe.

Society itself is more open toward sexual expression, so it is generally believed that sexual activity is a matter of individual choice. In his book *Out of the Shadows,* Patrick Carnes writes, "For the addict, however, there is no choice. No choice. The addiction is in charge. That addicts have no control over their sexual behavior is a very hard concept to accept when the addicts' trails have left broken marriages and parentless children, or worse, victims of sexual crimes. Therefore, there are no neutral responses to sexual compulsivity."[4]

What can we say about the addict?

First, he lives in constant fear of discovery; one of the strongest bonds is that of secrecy. Added to this is constant pain and alienation. "Addicts withhold a major portion of themselves—a pain deeply felt, but never expressed or witnessed."[5] Because they think that no one else is struggling as they do, they tend to internalize their addiction, condemning themselves yet unable to find a way out. They have an inner war that they think cannot be talked about.

Second, addicts do not become intimate with others, especially their families. Understandably, abandonment and shame are at the core of addiction. The members of the family, meanwhile, might suspect an addiction but would rather ignore it. The thought of having to deal with the implications of an addicted family member is more than they think they can bear. Their philosophy becomes "If you don't see it, it isn't there."

Third, the sex addict is constantly preoccupied with his particular habit. If he commits adultery, he enjoys the act, but he does not want a relationship. But fear of hurting his partners might make it difficult for him to break the relationship, so he hopes that his entanglements will just "go away" in and of themselves. But that doesn't happen, of course. He says, "I love you," to a woman, knowing full well that he said the same words to a different woman the night before.

Fourth, the addict often fantasizes about more risqué behavior. He might imagine meeting a strange woman at a bus stop, or wonder what it would be like to "rape" a woman in her own bedroom. Once a person has given himself over to fulfill his sexual desires, there is no telling where it all will end. His X-rated thought life becomes more and more detached from reality. His secret life becomes more real than his public life. Sexual addiction has this in common with other addictions: the addict is willing to risk everything—including those he loves—for a mood-altering experience of sexual euphoria.

The addict's fantasy life runs wild because he needs maximum sexual stimulation; each intoxicating experience has to reach the same (or a higher) level than the last. So the search, the suspense, the stolen must become a part of the arousal. Perhaps he will enter into a ritual to bring on the rush of excitement. The homosexual cruises, trying to find a partner in the same area as last time; the voyeur will walk past the same window where he saw a glimpse of an undressed woman, and now he receives a rush just by thinking about it.

Needless to say, addicts live with a deep level of denial, telling themselves that what they are doing is not ultimately harmful. After all, many others are doing the same—and worse. Or they will do many good deeds—taking care of their families or volunteering in church—trying to convince themselves that their addiction is only a small part of who they really are. At the core, they tell themselves, they are truly good, loving, and kind. What others don't know won't hurt them. A great deal of their energy is spent trying to give an outward veneer of normalcy and dependability. Some become masters at managing two separate lives. Sometimes only a crisis will jolt them back into the real world.

A man struggling with sexual addiction said to me, "I have struggled with sexual addiction for years and this is such a strong satanic stronghold. . . . I could not hear what my church or God was trying to tell me. Believe me when I say that most addicted men and women will listen to your words, but they will rationalize their behavior, just like I did for years." When the addict returns from his last experience, he will return home armed with a pack of carefully rehearsed lies so that the slightest suspicion is thwarted. If his wife does not believe him, he will angrily blame her for being jealous or "suspicious." Her feelings are her fault, not his.

Some addicts do not seek help until their lives fall apart and their secret life is exposed. Others, however, do want out and are willing to come into the light of truth on their own. Either way, we must be ready to help, encourage, and point the way to healing.

## FINDING THE WAY OUT

Perhaps you, like millions of Americans, are struggling with a sexual addiction, or you know someone who is. How can we walk the fine line of strong disapproval of illicit acts and still have compassion for the person who is caught in the trap of addiction? What do we need to know to offer both the cleansing and power of God?

Interestingly, women find it much more difficult to admit to sexual addiction. We expect that men, who are usually more sexually aggressive, would seek out multiple partners; but women are supposed to have their sexuality under control. But women who are abused and looking for love in all the wrong places might be just as bound to a lifestyle of meaningless serial relationships.

Whether one is having a "loving affair" or is addicted to serial relationships, the path to freedom is the same. There must be a humble recognition that offending God is never worth it; there must be an acknowledgment that no matter how secret the relationship, "Nothing in all creation is hidden from God's sight. Everything is uncovered and laid bare before the eyes of him to whom we must give account" (Hebrews 4:13).

Any sexual behavior can be rationalized by the mind except for one fact: that God is grieved by sexual sin. Only this can explain why Joseph was able to run from Potiphar's wife despite her enticements. His response: "How then could I do such a wicked thing and sin against God?" (Genesis 39:9). As long as we deal with men, sin can be hidden, excused, rationalized, and even glorified. But in the presence of a grieving God, our excuses fall away.

Even those who have learned to manage their guilt must come face-to-face with the reality of God's warnings and consolations. As for those who are Christians, they are grieving the Holy Spirit, who is living within them. Christ is present in the body of a Christian who commits indecent acts. That's why Paul asks, "Do you not know that your bodies are members of Christ himself? Shall I then take the members of Christ and unite them with a prostitute? Never!" (1 Corinthians 6:15). As Christians, we should not ask how we can manage living with our sin, but how we think Christ is able to manage living in us when we sin.

The addict does not struggle alone. Yes, there are others, many others, who have had the same level of obsession as he, and they have overcome it. There is no temptation or sin that is unique; it is common to the human race (1 Corinthians 10:13). Whenever I have heard a confession of sexual addiction, I have pointed out that such sin has existed since the beginning of the human race. The person sitting beside you in church or the man who works next to you in your office might be facing the same struggle as you. Your addiction does not make you less human but confirms the teaching of the Scriptures that apart from God's grace we are hapless people indeed.

There must be the assurance that if he comes clean there will be forgiveness and understanding, not judgment. His conscience has already condemned him a thousand times. His shame has locked him into his own world and held him hostage. Having lived in darkness, he must come to the light, where there is help and healing. He must be convinced that, yes, there is forgiveness for all sin—including sexual sins and, yes, even crimes.

Our churches must foster an attitude of acceptance, a humble spirit that encourages those who are locked in their secret world to come out from the shadows into the light. If secrecy and shame keep the addict bound, confession to those who can help is the path to true freedom. The tension between holding high standards and yet being gracious to the fallen must be humbly accepted.

So the weary struggler must be convinced that God is greater than his sordid past. Interestingly, the same Scripture that gives a stern warning about God's judgment against sexual sin combines it with hope.

*Do not be deceived: Neither the sexually immoral*
*nor idolaters nor adulterers nor male prostitutes*
*nor homosexual offenders nor thieves nor the greedy nor*
*drunkards nor slanderers nor swindlers will inherit the kingdom*
*of God. And that is what some of you were. But you were*
*washed, you were sanctified, you were justified in the name of*
*the Lord Jesus Christ and by the Spirit of our God.*

—1 CORINTHIANS 6:9–11

111

A former lesbian testified openly that the very idea of leaving that lifestyle was originally "an unthinkable thought." It was equivalent, she said, of being asked to lift a building by sheer willpower. If she had been asked to give up her lifestyle in order to become a Christian, it would have been impossible. Fortunately, she decided to come to Christ as she was and let Him help her change. With counseling and the encouragement of Christian friends, she was able to make the transition. She joins those in the first century who also experienced the power of God.

To those with various struggles, Paul says, "You were *washed*." Imagine the guilt, the shame, the lies all gone in the presence of a forgiving God. God begins by cleansing the unclean and restoring the numb consciences of those who have lived outside the boundaries of God's laws.

"You were *sanctified*," that is, set apart for God. If there is anything an addict needs to know, it is that all who come to Christ are precious to Him. To be "set apart" is to be given dignity, a sense of value. Christ sets us apart for Himself, wanting to do in and through us all that He desires.

"You were *justified*," that is, declared as righteous as Christ is! Imagine having God receive us just as He receives His Son! The issue is no longer the greatness of our sin, but the greatness of God's grace. "But where sin increased, grace increased all the more, so that, just as sin reigned in death, so also grace might reign through righteousness to bring eternal life though Jesus Christ our Lord" (Romans 5:20–21).

A rapist wrote me from prison asking if he too could be cleansed and forgiven. Though my first inclination was to say, "No!" I realized that God felt quite differently about the matter. So I wrote back and asked him to visualize two roads: one was quite well-traveled, with only a few ruts in the low spots. The other road was ugly, with ruts that led to the ditch and gravel strewn in unsightly heaps. But—and here is the good news—when a foot of snow falls, the roads cannot be distinguished from each other.

"'Come now, let us reason together,' says the Lord. 'Though your sins are like scarlet, they shall be as white as snow; though they are red as crimson, they shall be like wool'" (Isaiah 1:18). The ultimate question is not the greatness of our sins but the quality of the righteousness that covers them! Christ, who died for sinners, covers the sins of those who believe on Him. He invites us to have a new beginning.

A Lutheran minister told young pastors that they should always wear a clerical collar; it would keep them from sin, because it would be a reminder of who they really were. Although I don't care to wear clerical garb, the minister was making a telling point. If we remember who we are, we will be motivated to live up to our status. As a child of God, we should live up to expectations.

Keep in mind that overcoming an addiction is not an act but a process. When the addict's secret life is uncovered, he will usually experience a great deal of emotion; the knowledge that at last his hidden world is out in the open might be a relief. He might cry, make promises to reform, and express tenderness to those whom he has hurt. He will feel "clean," perhaps for the first time. At that moment he is unaware of the depth of his problem, for he now believes that he will never fall again. Now free from his guilt and shame, he looks upon his sexual escapades as something he can handle. He also will call to mind the many times when he did overcome temptation, and this will convince him that he is now free from his destructive behavior.

He is not. As the days go by, the desire to repeat the sexual trance intensifies. The rationalizations will again seek to take over. He will reason that if God could forgive him once, then he most assuredly can be forgiven again. He believes he will be successful in keeping his behavior from others—after all, he's had quite a bit of experience at secrecy. Thus, he will be strongly tempted to repeat his cycle. Repentance is not just one act done when we receive God's forgiveness; it is submission to God every single day, no matter how difficult the battle.

The memorization of Scripture, the life of prayer, and spiritual warfare—all of these are needed to maintain one's repentance. Personal accountability is so important. The addict needs a mentor who can ask him hard questions. Have you been looking at sexually explicit material? Have you been repeating the previously named sexual behavior? Have you been reading and memorizing Scripture? Just as an alcoholic has to be vigilant, knowing that he or she could repeat a drinking binge, so the sex addict must remember that as humans we always will be tempted to repeat the sin that once ensnared us.

Finally, the addict should, if possible, experience the healing of family relationships. His addiction has made intimacy impossible; shame and guilt have made him withdraw from those who are close to him. We have already explained that his addiction is probably rooted in a confused web of family relationships. Of course, sometimes it is impossible to rectify the dysfunctional family structure, but whenever possible this should be done.

If a marriage partner has committed adultery, it is important that there be counseling before reconciliation. There are issues of trust, communication, and accountability that are essential to restoration. These are not easy matters, and each situation is different. Perhaps one of the best books on the topic is *Torn Asunder: Recovering from Extramarital Affairs,* by David Carter.[6]

When Hosea's wife became a prostitute, symbolizing the spiritual adultery of the land of Judah, a promise was given to her:

> *"Therefore I am now going to allure her; I will lead her
> into the desert and speak tenderly to her. There I will give
> her back her vineyards, and will make the Valley of Achor
> a door of hope. There she will sing as in the days
> of her youth, as in the day she came up out of Egypt."*
>
> —HOSEA 2:14–15

God will do more than forgive the prostitute's sin. He will bring joy into her heart and make her sing as in the days of her virginity. She will not be a virgin in body but one in heart, mind, and spirit. God will give her a new beginning.

Psalm 51 is the heart cry of a fallen man who finally opened his life before God and let the light shine in. "The sacrifices of God are a broken spirit; a broken and contrite heart, O God, you will not despise" (v. 17). David the adulterer learned that there was grace even for those who have sinned in the face of unbounded mercy and great spiritual light.

114

## A PRAYER TO BEGIN THE JOURNEY

*"Have mercy on me, O God, according to your un-failing love; according to your great compassion blot out my transgressions. Wash away all my iniquity and cleanse me from my sin." (Read all of David's prayer of confession in Psalm 51.)*

*Father, forgive me for all the hurt I have caused others through my selfishness and sin. I pray that the desire to be in fellowship with You will be greater than the power of my shame and secrecy.*

*I have not only sinned against You, but against others: members of my family, my church, my illicit partner(s). I repent of all the lying and deception that has become so much a part of my lifestyle. By Your grace I will ask forgiveness of those I have wronged and be restored, as much as possible, to those who have been affected by my own sins.*

*I resist Satan. I stand against all the lies that I have so gladly believed and the lies I told to cover my sin. I acknowledge that I thought only about my pleasures and needs and did not consider the grief I caused You in my disobedience. I thank You that Jesus died not just to forgive me, but also to deliver me.*

*Let my repentance include accountability to those who can pray for me and stand with me in my temp-tations. Deliver me from evil. When I have the desire to repeat my sin, might I not have the opportunity; when I have the opportunity, may I not have the desire.*

*Give me the grace of restoration. Whatever the cost, may I be willing to "come clean" in confessing my failures to those who need to know. At all costs, let me be free because You have made me whole.*

*In Jesus' name, Amen.*

# THE SEARCH FOR PLEASURE: RUNNING ON EMPTY

*R*eflect on this statement: "You have to do what is best for yourself, so seek all the pleasure you can!"

At first blush, the remark seems wrong to its core. We live in a culture saturated with pleasure; we are a nation of pleasure seekers who shun deep thought about eternal values. We've already learned that addicts are created because of the natural human desire to seek gratification and avoid pain. And yet, we cannot escape the fact that all of us by nature seek pleasure, hoping to maximize happiness and minimize sadness.

Actually, seeking pleasure is not our problem; our temptation is to seek pleasure in all the wrong places. The addict cannot be faulted for seeking to fill his emptiness, but his deception is that he seeks fulfillment in places where it cannot be found. Or to put it differently, he seeks pleasures that in the end bring him more grief than bliss. And that is the problem with the wrong pleasures: they give the illusion of happiness, but in the end they bring bitterness, emptiness, and regret.

The Greeks were wise enough to know that we all seek pleasure.

They argued, quite correctly, that our motivation is happiness and that from our earliest experience we identify the good life with pleasure. A child tastes candy and says, "It is good," meaning, "It *tastes* good." Thus, we identify that which has a pleasant sensation with that which is good. Aristotle taught that happiness is being totally self-sufficient, and he went on to say that once we have attained happiness we do not look for anything else. In an ideal world, if we were completely happy, we would lack nothing. But since life is far from ideal, we spend our lives seeking pleasure and avoiding pain.

Christian thinkers agree that seeking pleasure is not in itself wrong; indeed, we are so constituted that we cannot do otherwise. As Pascal wrote, "All look for happiness without exception. Although they use different means, they all strive toward this objective. That is why some go to war and some do other things. So this is the motive for every deed of man, including those who hang themselves. . . . So he vainly searches, but finds nothing to help him, other than to see an infinite abyss that can only be filled by One who is Infinite and Immutable. In other words, it can only be filled by God himself."[1]

Our task, then, is to search for the greater pleasure, not the lesser; we should strive for the permanent, not the temporary. Obviously God is not opposed to our seeking the pleasures that are found in Him. "You have made known to me the path of life; you will fill me with joy in your presence, with eternal pleasures at your right hand" (Psalm 16:11).

A great snare, perhaps the greatest of the snares, is the futile hope that our raging thirst for fulfillment can be met by the pleasures of this world. Our temptation is to love that which is vain, that which is empty. By nature we drink water from the wrong fountain and eat bread from the wrong table. And in the process we fall victim to one of the devil's most believable lies.

Even if we have escaped alcoholism, even if we have escaped the lure of pornography, we might find ourselves standing helplessly before the goddess of pleasure, listening to her cries and wanting to believe her promises. We do not need to be addicted to gambling in order to grieve God; all that we need to do is to be absorbed with personal ambition, setting our sights on the here and now rather than pursuing those pleasures that gladden God's heart.

Neil Postman writes that at different times in our history, different cities have been the focal point of radiating the American spirit. In the late eighteenth century, Boston was the center of political radicalism; in the mid-nineteenth century, New York became the symbol of melting-pot America; Chicago, the city of big shoulders, came to symbolize the industrial energy and dynamism of America. Today, however, says Postman,

> We must look to Las Vegas, Nevada, as a metaphor of our national character and aspiration, its symbol a thirty-foot-high cardboard picture of a slot machine and a chorus girl. For Las Vegas is entirely devoted to the idea of entertainment, and as such proclaims the spirit of a culture in which all public discourse increasingly takes the form of entertainment. Our politics, religion, news, athletics, education and commerce have been transformed into congenial adjuncts of show business. The result is that we are a people on the verge of amusing ourselves to death.[2]

Postman is primarily concerned about television, not because it is entertaining but because "it has made entertainment itself the natural format for the representation of all experience. . . . The problem is not that television presents us with entertaining subject matter but that all subject matter is presented as entertaining, which is another issue altogether."[3] He makes the point, which all of us have witnessed, that in the middle of a most serious news story—the war in Bosnia, for example—the account is interrupted with "a series of commercials that will, in an instant, defuse the import of the news, in fact, render it largely banal."[4] He argues that there are some matters that demand such thought and analysis that television of necessity will do them an injustice; it is not capable of handling serious subjects.

We're not listening to Postman, of course. Today everything is made to fit the television mode. We use an entertainment medium that by its very nature cannot do serious matters justice. We are accustomed to be amused, and we will be amused even in the midst of the atrocities that dot our planet.

As for television programming itself, when a rating system was adopted a few years ago, many predicted that it would worsen an already bad TV lineup. As feared, the warning labels have only provided a cover for even raunchier programming. Since the ratings were instituted, sex, profanity, violence, and assorted kinds of immorality have soared. Even the so-called "family hour" has been invaded by an increase in offensive programs. Add to this the many degrading talk shows and you have a virtual river of impurity flowing into our homes. When TV executives pander to the pleasures of this world, they will always appeal to the basest of human cravings. We identify with the wag who said, "I can get 57 channels but there's nothing on."

This preoccupation with this world's pleasure is called *hedonism*. This is the life of sex, food, money, leisure, and consumption of all kinds. This lifestyle values a "this world" mentality; the assumption is that we exist to serve ourselves and all that implies. People are looking for an escape, something to get away from the pressures of work and unhealthy social relationships. They are also looking for something to fill their "raging thirst." But, alas, it is not to be.

You'd think that the following words were written in the twenty-first century: "But mark this: There will be terrible times in the last days. People will be lovers of themselves, lovers of money, boastful, proud, abusive, disobedient to their parents, ungrateful, unholy, without love, unforgiving, slanderous, without self-control, brutal, not lovers of the good, treacherous, rash, conceited, lovers of pleasure rather than lovers of God—having a form of godliness but denying its power. Have nothing to do with them" (2 Timothy 3:1–5). *Lovers of pleasure rather than lovers of God!*

When man is left to himself, he will always gravitate to the basest of desires. Yes, he will love himself rather than God and find his delight in the creature, not the Creator. He will opt for the pleasure that promises the greatest sensation *today*.

## THE WORLD WE SHOULD NOT LOVE

We must distinguish three different uses of the word "world" in Scripture. Sometimes it refers to this planet, that is, the world that God created. We speak of God's creating the world, and we are reminded that we should take care of this planet. Unfortunately, the environmental movement of today is often combined with a New Age theology and concerns about "Mother Earth" and the like. But there is a proper kind of environmentalism: a fundamental commitment to take care of the resources God has created.

The word "world" is often used for the world of people, the world that God loves. One day when our oldest daughter was but a child she asked me if we should love everyone, even if they are evil. When I replied, "Yes," she said, "Well, that means we should love Satan too!" Well, not so fast! There is this difference: Christ died to redeem those who would believe on Him, but Satan was not included in that sacrifice. Because he sinned against such light, we are to regard him as God's evil enemy. No, we don't love him, for this would be a love that God hates. People, *yes;* the devil, *no!*

And finally, "the world" is often used to refer to a whole system of values and attitudes of a society that has abandoned God. When we hear the phrase "the world of sports," we know that it does not refer to a separate planet but to an organized system of ideas and various competitive events. Just so, "the world" is often used in the Scriptures to refer to a system of ideas and attitudes; it refers to hedonistic values and a fundamental commitment to this life in contrast to the next. At its worst, it is assigning high values to what God condemns; at its best, it is rearranging the price tags. If you want to know what the world is, just surf through the channels on your television set.

By any measure, evangelist Dwight L. Moody was one of the most influential evangelists in the world. His work, centered here in Chicago, was begun by winning neglected children to Christ. It is said that through his preaching he "shook two continents for God," the British Isles and America. Others have pointed out that through the founding of the Moody Bible Institute and the Moody Church, he has "shaken the world for God." One of his favorite verses was 1 John 2:15–17. In the NIV it reads: "Do not love the world or anything in the world. If anyone loves the world, the love of the Father is not in him. For everything in the world—the cravings of sinful man, the lust of his eyes and the boasting of what he has and does—comes not from the Father but from the world. The world and its desires pass away, but the man who does the will of God lives forever."

What can we say about this world that we are warned we should not love?

First, it is controlled by Satan. He is "the god of this world" (2 Corinthians 4:4 NASB). Behind the pleasures of the world lies the being whom we introduced in previous chapters, the devil, who seeks our destruction. Of course the world would be tempting to us even if Satan did not exist, but it is he who has tried to organize opposition to God and tries to draw us into his ingenious plans.

Second, the world is seductive because it is presented to us as the "natural" thing to do to meet our personal needs. Our God-given desire for pleasure is co-opted by the deceptive pleasures of this life that offer so much but in the end reward us so badly. It is sugar sweetly poisoned. The world we are not to love is the world of desire—the world of lust and a covetous heart. This surely is our most subtle snare.

Let's reflect on the three aspects John mentions in the verse quoted above.

## The Cravings of Sinful Man

The pleasures of this world and the pleasures of God collided when Christian college students descended on Panama City Beach for spring break. The *Chicago Tribune* reported that these students "bowed their heads, closed their eyes and concentrated on how best to compete with bikinis, beer bongs and the booming bass that blared from Chevy Suburbans cruising 'the strip' in what is widely recognized as the spring break capital of the world."[5]

Revelers carrying 12-packs of Bud Light under their arms and en route to a wet T-shirt contest and beach volleyball games were, for the most part, woefully disinterested in being evangelized. When the Christian students asked them whether they would go to heaven if they died tomorrow, some of them listened politely but then walked away. Many said they were not concerned about what would happen to them tomorrow. How could they, with their beers and girls waiting? This was not the time to reflect on some distant pleasures. Today was all that mattered.

Such pleasures deceive us, for they give the illusion of fulfillment and happiness, yet, for all their promises, leave us empty, guilty, and unfulfilled. In the end, they rob us of the satisfaction that comes from knowing we have pleased the Lord. The world is not neutral, asking us to make of it what we will. From God's point of view, it is our enemy, a seductive influence we must always resist.

"What good is it for a man to gain the whole world, yet forfeit his soul? Or what can a man give in exchange for his soul?" (Mark 8:36–37).

A woman whom we shall call Ann was reared in a Christian home, but when she found herself in an unfulfilling marriage she became disillusioned with Christianity. When she sought advice from other Christians, she received sympathy and even pity, but no help. She reluctantly drifted to an inescapable conclusion: except perhaps for a few pastors and missionaries, it was impossible to live the Christian life.

Ann began to think that the world was not as bad as she had been told it was. How could she know? She had never tried it. Soap operas began to fill the vacuum in her life. Her own marriage was a drag in comparison to the excitement of the daytime programs. There was a world out there she wanted to sample, to find out for herself what it was like. To meet her deep needs she had an affair, secretly savoring the taste of "forbidden fruit." As many others have discovered, sin has its pleasures. She found her new relationship exhilarating. But as the weeks progressed, she had to fight against the guilt and emptiness of it all. She pushed thoughts about God out of her mind, telling herself that she would deal with the Almighty "somewhere down the road."

She faced a choice: should she pursue the pleasure of self-gratification or the pleasures that come through obedience to God? Thankfully, her liaison was discovered, and she ended her relationship. Her marriage would have been destroyed were it not for the fact that she and her husband worked through the betrayal, the accusations, and the grief her actions had caused. She is an example of someone of whom James Allen is quoted as saying: "From the state of a man's heart proceed the conditions of his life; his thoughts blossom into deeds and his deeds bear the fruitage of character and destiny"[6]

Make no mistake: the world tells us that the pleasure of following

God cannot begin to compare with the unrelenting titillation of self-gratification. "Do not love the world," John wrote, knowing full well that we will put our affections somewhere. We all have what C. S. Lewis called "an overwhelming first." Talk to anyone for more than a few moments, ask the right questions, and his first love(s) will soon surface. Pleasure will always compete with our love for Christ. This passion for pleasure can only be subdued by a greater passion for Him.

## The Lust of His Eyes

Yes, the eyes can have an appetite. We sometimes say, "Just fix your eyes on this . . ." When John described the world as "the lust of [the] eyes," he might have been referring to sensual temptation, but more likely it was the sin of covetousness that he had in mind. We've already discussed greed in a previous chapter, but I must make a few comments here about consumerism.

Our problem is not that we consume in order to live, but that too often we live in order to consume. "Consumerism," writes Rodney Clapp, "is an ethos, a character-cultivating way of life that seduces and insinuates and acclimates. This, too often, is consumption that militates against the Christian virtues of patience, contentedness, self-denial and generosity—almost always with a velvet glove rather than an iron fist. It speaks in sweet and sexy rather than dictatorial tones, and it conquers by promises rather than by threats."[7] *Yes, this velvet glove conquers by promises rather than threats!*

Our spiritual forefathers would not have agreed with our unqualified endorsement of our capitalistic/consumer-oriented way of life. The author of a first-century document called the Didache wrote, "Never turn away the needy; share all your possessions with your brother, and do not claim that anything is your own. If you and he are joint participators in things immortal, how much more so in things that are mortal?"[8] And another first-century document gave this counsel: "Instead of fields, then, buy souls that are in trouble. . . . Look after widows and orphans and do not neglect them. Spend your riches and all your establishments you have received from God on this kind of field and houses."[9]

Consumerism is but another kind of hedonism. Advertisers are constantly creating new needs for us. Above all, they insist that we cannot be satisfied with what we have, or our penchant for their products would come to an end. The world tells us that we must constantly be in a state of dissatisfaction so that we will want to buy more and increase the variety and intensity of our experiences. The game is to keep fulfillment and satisfaction just beyond our reach.

Of course it would be easy for me to speak about how much money Americans spend on skiing in Colorado; how much we spend on conveniences we really don't need; how much we waste on pornography, sex, movies, sports, and so on. I could comment on the money spent by believers to own a second home at the beach, and how some people keep a condo in Florida. But the matter is more subtle than that: we can love anything to the detriment of our love for God. "Our heart," said Calvin, "is an idol factory." We are constantly setting our affections on the things of this world, rather than on God. We are in continual danger of breaking the commandment "You shall have no other gods before me" (Exodus 20:3).

The person mesmerized by the Chicago Bulls; the person in love with the arts; the woman forever obsessed with the finer pleasures of eating and shopping—such individuals might also be idolaters to the core. Ezekiel the prophet spoke God's word to those who "set up their idols in their hearts" (Ezekiel 14:3 NASB). Our problem is that the world is so much a part of our thinking that it is hard for us to even identify "worldliness" in our lives. If we are honest, we will find it not just around us but in us. We are like a fish swimming in the river but seemingly unaware of the water.

## The Boasting of What He Has and Does

The third motivation of the world is the crowning of the self, that basic commitment to have our world revolve around our desires, interests, and needs. For those who are born with a natural physical attractiveness, there is the temptation to flaunt beauty and take pride in appearance. In the list of seven sins God hates, "a proud look" stands at the head (Proverbs 6:17 KJV).

Serving one's self is the core of worldliness. Even if we don't brag about ourselves, we would like to. We especially like to compare ourselves with those who are shy of our attainments. We are tempted, says one, to have pride of *face, race,* and *grace.* We find it difficult to delight in the successes of others; we are more concerned about our portfolio than we are the single mother across the street.

Workaholism is often a symptom of the NASB reading, "the boastful pride of life." We crave to be recognized, to be thought of as successful, and to put our mark on the world. Since we don't think we are appreciated by our families, who don't share our values, we invest our energy where we will get the most recognition and where we will finally be successful. We also want to be in a position financially where we can be disconnected from the pain and suffering of the poor.

We have to ask ourselves some tough questions: Do our "good deeds" spring from a love for God or, perhaps, from a subtle love of self? Perhaps the real reason I give a five dollar bill to a beggar is not because I have a genuine concern for his need but because it makes me feel good. I think of myself as a better person because I took the time and made the small sacrifice to help someone beneath me on the social ladder; in fact, I can tell my wife about it that evening. Quite frankly, this is why acts of charity are often made public; people like to be recognized for their contributions.

Jesus told a parable about four different kinds of soil. In the first category, the seed that fell along the path was eaten by the birds. In the second instance, the seed fell among rocks and germinated, but because it had no roots, vanished away. The third kind of soil is perhaps the most applicable: "Still others, like seed sown among thorns, hear the word; but the worries of this life, the deceitfulness of wealth and the desires for other things come in and choke the word, making it unfruitful" (Mark 4:18–19). *The deceitfulness of wealth and the desires for other things choke the word, making it unfruitful.*

The cravings of sinful man, the lust of the eyes, and boasting—these are not the pleasures for which we were created. They are found in the wrong things, and they will not endure. The pleasures of this world are in line with the basest of our motives and eschew sacrifice. And they cloud our relationship with God. Worse, they grieve Him.

These pleasures deceive us because they make promises they cannot keep. We seek them, but they are never really satisfying. They are not what they appear to be. They are wrapped in the wrong paper; they are the path of least resistance; they ask us to sacrifice the permanent on the altar of the immediate. They prevent us from enjoying the pleasures of God. Paul, when speaking about widows who use their singleness as an excuse for flirtatious behavior, says, "But the widow who lives for pleasure is dead even while she lives" (1 Timothy 5:6). In the world, all the wells are dry.

Robert Burns was right when he wrote:

> But pleasures are like poppies spread—
> You seize the flow'r its bloom is shed
> Or like the snow falls in the river—
> A moment white then melts forever.

## THE PLEASURES OF GOD

But weren't we created to enjoy some pleasures? The opera, the sunset, the arts; the genuine beauty? My wife loves flowers and derives strength from the beauty of the mountains and trees. Yet even these pleasures can be deceptive if they are enjoyed without relation to God. As Christians we should enjoy creation differently; for us, the heavens are not just wonderful but "declare the glory of God" (Psalm 19:1). In creation, God went public. The wonder of nature in the work of the Father and the Son is "the spilling over of their mutual joy."[10] Yes, we can delight in the opera, works of art, and beauty, because these are the means by which we praise Him. "O LORD, how manifold are thy works! in wisdom hast thou made them all" (Psalm 104:24 KJV).

Our choice is stark and urgent. Just ask Moses.

*By faith Moses, when he had grown up, refused to be known as the son of Pharaoh's daughter. He chose to be mistreated along with the people of God rather than to enjoy the pleasures of sin for a short time. He regarded disgrace for the sake of Christ as of greater value than the treasures of Egypt, because he was looking ahead to his reward. By faith he left Egypt, not fearing the king's anger; he persevered because he saw him who is invisible.*

—HEBREWS 11:24–27

According to Josephus, Moses was next in line to be Pharaoh, and in those days rulers were deified and worshiped with ceremony and devotion. Many of us did not know what the treasures of Egypt were until King Tut's tomb was brought here to Chicago. The Pharaohs had more wealth than you can imagine. They had more personal pleasure than you could dream about. Hundreds of servants, hundreds of women, and hundreds of ways to satisfy their every craving. Yes, he could have had it all.

Moses threw it all away. Measured by any worldly standard, he was a fool. But in the eyes of God and the eyes of anyone else who mattered, he was a mighty wise man. He saw the fleeting pleasures of sin for what they were. He knew that there would be a tomorrow; he knew there would be an eternity, and he chose to weigh his decision on the balance. The pleasure of women would be gone. The pleasure of luxury would be gone. The pleasure of power would be gone.

The choice was not between pleasure and no pleasure; the choice was between the pleasures of this world and the pleasures of the next. It was between what he could have had in the palace and what he experienced in the desert. He took a hard look at his options and knew which one would be best for God, but also best for him. *He regarded disgrace for the sake of Christ of greater value than the treasures of Egypt because he was looking ahead to his reward!*

What would we be saying about Moses today if he had chosen Egypt? He would have been another footnote to history. Today he is an example of a man who lived for all the right reasons. If Peter, James, or John, who joined him briefly on the Mount of Transfiguration, had asked him if they thought he had made the right decision, what do you think he would have said?

Where would you and I be today if Jesus had chosen personal pleasure rather than the route to the cross? "Let us fix our eyes on Jesus, the author and perfecter of our faith, who for the joy set before him endured the cross, scorning its shame, and sat down at the right hand of the throne of God" (Hebrews 12:2). If you have ever been fired from a job because you are honest; if you have ever been bypassed for a promotion because of your Christian witness; if you have had to say no to some pleasures in order to say yes to God—be thankful that you stand with the likes of Moses and Jesus, who turned

128

aside from the here and now to do something that will count in the hereafter.

Are you facing a tough decision? Are you working on a budget to allocate your income? Are you debating how to use the time you still have left in this world? Ask yourself a simple question: A century from now what decision will you wish you had made? Once you answer that, your decision is made. Only such choices can stand the test of time. Peter Marshall wrote,

> Once and for all, we must put out of our minds that the purpose of life here is to enjoy ourselves
> > to have a good time
> > to be happy
> > to make money
> > and to live in ease and comfort.
> That is not what life is all about. You were put here for a purpose, and that purpose is not related to superficial pleasures.
> No one owes you a living—not your parents, not your government, not life itself.
> You do not have a right to happiness.
> You have a right to nothing.
> I believe that God wants us to be happy—but it is not a matter of our *right*, but of his *love and mercy*.[11]

All of us know the impact of the life of Cassie Bernall, who was shot to death in the terrible massacre in the Columbine High School shootings. Seventeen-year-old Cassie, the story goes, was asked by one of the shooters during the massacre if she believed in God. She paused for a second, not because she doubted her faith, but because she knew what her faith might cost her. She replied, "Yes, and you should too." With that, bullets riddled her body.

Was her answer a wise one? Richard Roper, in an editorial piece in the *Chicago Sun Times,* argues it wasn't. He laments the fact that her answer turned her into a pop martyr. He asks, "What if she had said, 'I don't believe in God'?" Though it is impossible to know that such a statement would have saved her life, would that have been a proper response?

He admits that there is nothing really wrong with elevating her to sainthood, to the role of a religious martyr. But he is concerned that she be thought more valuable than the other children who died.

Then he concludes:

> Admirable. Wonderful. Incredibly brave. But let's not for a moment believe that any of the victims who didn't respond to the God question or perhaps were not asked about their faith are somehow less deserving of a place in heaven.
>
> What if Cassie had said no? Would that have made her less of a person?
>
> I don't think so, and much more to the point, I'd like to believe God wouldn't think so. If a girl just beginning her adult life has a chance to survive by lying to a twisted sicko pointing a gun at her—if she can not only win her own future but spare those who love her the anguish of losing her—maybe she should take that chance. Call me blasphemous for saying so and quote Scripture to me until you are blue in the face, but I ask you: If it were your son or daughter on the wrong end of that gun and a simple "no" could make a difference, what would you hope your child would say?[12]

Well, what do you wish your son or daughter would say? It is not an easy answer if a simple "no" would spare our life. But it all depends on how much value you place on the other world. It depends on how much you believe in eternity. The martyrs of the past answered that question, and the promise to them was "Be faithful, even to the point of death, and I will give you the crown of life" (Revelation 2:10).

It was the devil who said to God, "A man will give all he has for his own life" (Job 2:4). As always, the devil was lying. Many people have believed that there are some values that are worth more than life itself; there are still some things worth dying for. Evidently Cassie believed that too.

## YOUR RESPONSE

Given our affluent culture, most of us grew up with enough money and opportunity to fulfill many of our selfish pleasures. Apart from the need to earn a living, we are able to do practically whatever we like, whether it be travel, movies, hobbies, and the like. We can live in a fine home insulated from the quiet desperation of those who live in our cities, or for that matter, insulated from the hurting family next door. We stand in desperate need of repentance.

In his book *The Way of the Heart,* Henri Nouwen quotes Thomas Merton as saying that the "desert fathers" believed that society was "a shipwreck from which each single individual man had to swim for his life. . . . These were men who believed that to let oneself drift along, passively accepting the tenets and values of what they knew as society, was purely and simply a disaster."[13] We might not agree that we should return to the solitude of the desert, but it might be time for us to turn off our television sets, give our surplus money to missions, and quite literally seek the Lord with all our hearts.

You've heard it said that the problem with the church in Laodicea was that it was self-satisfied with its lukewarmness. But its condition was far worse than that: Lukewarmness has an effective cure called *repentance.* The problem with the church was that *it was lukewarm but thought it was hot.* Read the Lord's diagnosis carefully. "You say, 'I am rich; I have acquired wealth and do not need a thing.' *But you do not realize that you are wretched, pitiful, poor, blind and naked"* (Revelation 3:17, italics added). Only God knows the extent to which we have been filling our lives with selfish gratification. And only He can show us our true condition.

Here are three decisions we must make:

First, to commit our funds to God and genuinely recognize them as His, with all that implies. Rodney Clapp was right when he wrote, "Consumerism will continue to exercise undue influence over Christians until we desecrate this unholy taboo and stop regarding our economic lives as an entirely private matter, finding ways to open our wallets and checkbooks in front of trusted Christians."[14]

Second, we must give our discretionary time to God, vowing to turn off our TV and ask, "Lord, what will you have me to do?" The organizing principle of our lives must be a love for God and the evangelism of those who do not know Christ as Savior. In short, we must leave the world behind and begin to fulfill the mandate the Lord has given to us.

Finally, our commitment must penetrate deeply within our hearts. "Above all else, guard your heart, for it is the wellspring of life" (Proverbs 4:23). Only when we are intoxicated with God will we be inoculated against the world.

## A PRAYER TO BEGIN THE JOURNEY

*Father, I thank You that Jesus our High Priest has prayed for us, "My prayer is not that you take them out of the world but that you protect them from the evil one. They are not of the world, even as I am not of it. Sanctify them by the truth; your word is truth" (John 17:15–17). Today I pray that You will reveal all the worldliness that has a grip on my heart. Show me what You see and give me the gift of repentance.*

*I transfer to You all my fleshly desires; I affirm that You, through Jesus, have made it possible for me to "live by the Spirit" so that I do not have to fulfill the desires of the flesh (Galatians 5:16, 25; Ephesians 2:3). I surrender all that I own to You; I choose to rejoice in what You have given to others, and I stand against the deceptions that Satan puts in my path. Take from me a prideful spirit and grant me the grace to walk before You in humility.*

*Give me wisdom as to how I can use my time wisely; help me to remember that we have been left here to tell others of Your love and forgiveness. Break all bondages that hinder me from sharing my faith with a world that is headed for destruction.*

*Show me each day how I can say no to the world You hate and yes to the Savior I love.*

*In Jesus' name, Amen.*

# OCCULTISM: SUPERSTITION OR DECEPTION?

The two shooters of the Columbine tragedy were enamored with Adolf Hitler, which might explain why the massacre took place on his birthday. That is significant, not only because Hitler is one of the most notorious men in history, but also because he was deeply involved in what we call the occult—the world of darkness, superstition, and demonic powers. No wonder that a man who knew Hitler said that "his body was but the shell for the spirit that inhabited him."

The lure of the occult is everywhere—in television, the Internet, bookstores, and movies. Although at one time it existed on the fringe of society, today it is mainstream. This snare beckons us with the bait of curiosity, secret knowledge, fulfillment, and power. And there are as many different lures as there are interests among the masses. Today, occultism is no longer disguised but exists openly for all to see.

From ancient times, men have wanted to peer into the spirit world without regard to the teachings and safeguards of the Bible. Our innate desire to connect with a greater power has made the human race interested in the unseen world, with its promise of fulfillment.

Satan, of course, is willing to oblige, for his greatest desire is to take the place of God. Think of his momentary delight when people encounter him but think they are in contact with the true and living God!

We sometimes hear, "God has a wonderful plan for your life." But we can also say, "Satan has a *destructive* plan for your life." He has already made meticulous plans for your downfall. Though any snare can undo us, the occult is his most brazen attempt to recruit us for his kingdom.

Animals usually don't get caught by accident; they are lured into circumstances that look attractive but conceal a deadly hook. We've already learned that it would be foolish to think we could catch a mouse without a trap; mice only see the cheese and do not understand the wire and the powerful spring. Likewise, when Satan lays a snare for us, he himself remains hidden; if not, we would be frightened. Most of the entry points seem harmless enough, but when we walk through the door we find ourselves trapped on the other side.

Satan tries to develop a keen understanding of his victims. Just as we know that fish prefer worms to cheese, so Satan knows our weaknesses and habits. He and his demons are keen observers of human nature. He also knows where we work and our special secrets—those attitudes and behaviors that we keep from others. That provides him and his emissaries with the most fruitful area of temptation.

Satan begins by injecting thoughts into our minds that we think are our own, just as he did with Ananias (Acts 5:3). That is brilliant strategy, because although sin is attractive to believers, Satan is not. If he were to appear to us, we would be terrified, but because we think our thoughts are wholly our own, we have no fear. In this chapter we can do little more than survey a few of the snares of the occult and sketch the path to victory.

## RECRUITMENT IN MOVIES AND TELEVISION

Doorways into the occult exist everywhere. But television and movies cast the widest net and capture the greatest number of recruits. Television shows such as *Buffy the Vampire Slayer* and *Charmed* and movies such as *Practical Magic* and *The Craft* make the occult popular. Many people attend these kinds of movies or watch these television programs and see them as harmless and cute. But they are loaded with occult messages and lures.

In an article titled "Weird Sisters," Margaret Kim Peterson explains how these shows portray witchcraft as a kind of pantheistic nature religion. Witches in the movie *The Craft* announce, "We worship everything; God, the devil, the earth, trees."[1] One of the witches in *Practical Magic* explains that witchcraft has to do with being close to nature. Witchcraft is accompanied by many accessories: candles, occult symbols, brooms, potions, and books on how to cast spells. These young witches evoke the power of the wind and the trees.

What do witches get in exchange for these charms? They have a variety of paranormal powers, such as levitation, psychic power to see the future, and the ability to manipulate the thoughts of others or to destroy certain kinds of evil. Sometimes they have to defend themselves against an occult power that has gone wrong.

There is a downside to being a witch. Sometimes these powers are hard to control; witches are often misunderstood and rejected. So they have to conceal and lie about their vocation. And yet it is not easy to opt out of being a witch because certain people are born into it. Some grow up and only later discover that they were born to be witches. What is important is that they accept their differences, for as Peterson points out, "Not accepting yourself is the original sin in these media tales of witchcraft."

From these shows we learn that witchcraft is passed from mother to daughter. As one of the sisters in *Charmed* notes, "It's a chick thing—it's passed down the female line." Thus, these witches discover that their mothers were witches before them. The bonds of witchcraft are passed along through blood rituals, and witches are often banded together by a curse. Thus they are called upon to exorcise demons, though they are both glad and apprehensive about doing so.

These witches have all experienced abuse at the hands of men. They desire the love of a man, but they are deeply afraid that men will abuse them or abandon them. Thus their relationship with men turns seductive and murderously angry. They are filled with revenge for the evil that men have done to them. The sisters in *Charmed* were abandoned as children by their father. They all behave seductively toward men but their relationships are always abusive; the witches must protect themselves, for the men always try to take advantage of them.

The sisters in *Practical Magic* come from a long line of witches who live under a curse pronounced by a foremother who was abandoned by her lover. The curse stipulates that any man they love will die an untimely death. When one sister falls in love, it is with a man who beats her and tries to murder her. "It takes an entire coven to vanquish this man once and for all, and when he has been finally destroyed, one of the witches turns to the other and says, 'I wonder if that would work on my ex-husband.'"[2]

What is the theology of these shows? Peterson points out that in them God is one of several comparable spiritual entities; He is seen as there along with nature, or perhaps as being one with nature. No one is ultimately in charge of what happens in the world. As a woman who runs a witchcraft supply store in *The Craft* explains, "Magic is neither good nor bad; it is both, because nature is both." The spiritual dimensions are presented as powerful, but if a person is careful and has good intentions, he can use it in sort of a way for that which is good. "There is no sense that any spiritual entity might be either so evil or so holy that it would be foolhardy to have anything to do with it."[3]

Human beings are presented as basically good, though some are evil. The line between good and evil runs through the human race, not through the human heart. Good people make mistakes, as when witches fail to use their powers or use their powers to do self-centered things such as winning the lottery. But those who are good should use their powers to destroy those who are bad.

To summarize their view of human nature, "While the bad deserve and receive violent death, good human beings deserve and receive fullness of life, which consists largely of being young and beautiful, having a lot of sex, and owning lots of things. Good people are never poor, old, unattractive, or chaste. These are the predicaments from which the witches rescue people; they are not consonant with life as it ought to be."[4]

"In such a scenario" writes Peterson, "it is not surprising that redemption is missing. In all of these shows, the good people do not need to be redeemed and the bad people cannot be. So the good need simply to be rewarded, the evil people punished. There is no forgiveness, no grace, no possibility of change."[5]

Perhaps we can better understand why these movies are so appealing. Many young women can identify with having been either abused or at least misused by men. Since men are going to abandon you, the reasoning goes, the only lasting relationships can come through friendship with women. What is more, becoming a witch with the power to cast spells and wreak havoc is an inviting way to get back at the male species. Human justice says that they are getting what they deserve.

At a time when our homes are in disarray and men do abuse women, it is easy to see why these shows touch an emotional cord. Just think how enticing all of this might be to abused teenagers, who feel that they must protect themselves from the hurts of this world by connecting to some power that is greater than themselves.

Witchcraft is also attractive in an age that worships the self. "While witchcraft sees evil as a dangerous reality, it locates evil outside of the self. There is no sense of sin in witchcraft. . . . It enables its practitioners to combat the evil forces in the universe and in their lives, but it does not suggest there is anything about the witch herself that needs fixing—except, perhaps, that she is not yet sufficiently true to herself." Thus, "spiritual reality is whatever a witch wants it to be; it is neither good nor bad in itself, but is waiting to be used by anyone willing to pay the price to tap into this enormous power."[6]

Peterson concludes, "Far from challenging human devotion to consumerism, sex, violence, and individual fulfillment, witchcraft is just one more way of having just what one wants, and having it now."[7] Anton LaVey, founder of the church of Satan, said, "This is a very selfish religion. We believe in greed, we believe in selfishness, we believe in all of the lustful thoughts that motivate man, because this is man's natural feeling."[8]

Just surf your television channels if you have any doubt that movies are laced with occultic rituals and references. Millions of teenagers, along with many adults, find themselves intrigued, curious, and finally drawn into some kind of involvement. Satan plays by no rules, so he will impose his darkness on anyone who comes near his realm. Telltale signs of those affected are mood swings, morbid introspection, and isolation from others. Our enemy does his most daring work when we are alone, inwardly focused, and willing to investigate the darkness. And the more we dabble in his playpen, the more hopeless we are of turning back.

## OTHER PATHS TO SATAN'S DOOR

We can make contact with Satan's kingdom through films, or we could join a coven, practice blood rituals, or sell our soul to the devil. But for the average American, none of these ways is appealing. Most people enter through mainstream self-help techniques that in the end result in the same bondage and demonic involvement. They come into the occult in ways that have a more inviting label.

Truth, despite all of its awesome power for good, has one glaring disadvantage: there is only one way to be right, but many ways to be wrong. Two plus two equals four. Only one number satisfies the equation, but false answers are endless. There is only one way to be right, but many ways to be wrong! Satan has as many ways to deceive people as there are interests among the masses. He can use religion, health fads, pseudoscience, and a host of other curious seeds that will eventually bear bitter fruit.

## Astrology

What is necessary for a technique or practice to lead to the darker side of the spirit world? Just one: It must violate the first commandment, "You shall have no other gods before me" (Exodus 20:3). Thus, any object that purports to give supernatural guidance violates that commandment, for the Scriptures teach that we should look to the true God for direction in our lives. In Isaiah 47:12–15, God angrily taunts the Babylonians for their reliance on astrology:

> *Keep on, then, with your magic spells and with your many*
> *sorceries, which you have labored at since childhood.*
> *Perhaps you will succeed, perhaps you will cause terror.*
> *All the counsel you have received has only worn you out!*
> *Let your astrologers come forward, those stargazers who make*

*predictions month by month, let them save you from*
*what is coming upon you. Surely they are like stubble;*
*the fire will burn them up. They cannot even save*
*themselves from the power of the flame. . . . Each of them*
*goes on in his error; there is not one that can save you.*

*Just dial this number for a free psychic hotline reading!* We've all heard and seen the ads on television that invite tarot readings. What follows are personal testimonies of people whose lives were changed because they spoke to someone who could foresee their fortunes and misfortunes, their impending romances and vocational opportunities. And, thanks to human ingenuity, they were able to take advantage of the hidden knowledge. Of course sometimes these "prophets" got it right. If you make enough predictions, you will not be wrong every time. Some of these psychics can see into the future as far as the devil who controls them can; others are just charlatans. Whatever, God is not amused.

Astrology is an abomination because it bypasses God in the search for wisdom; in effect, it is shaking one's fist in the face of the Almighty. Ouija boards, horoscopes, fortune-telling, and other such practices violate this basic principle. They are appealing snares that lead the unwary into submission to occult phenomena controlled by the Enemy (Deuteronomy 18: 9–14).

## New Age Healing

Any practice or object that claims supernatural power to heal (either physically or emotionally) is also a substitute for faith in the one true God. Crystals and psychic therapies that use "healing guides" make such claims. Millions of Americans are now combining nutrition and psychic or spiritual experiences to create a "holistic" approach to health. This fad tries to combine the mind sciences with physical science to achieve a sense of well-being. Teachings derived from Eastern philosophies are deftly mixed with legitimate information on good health. There are lectures on reflexology, visualization, and self-hypnosis. I've collected brochures featuring some of the seminars available, such as *Awakening the Healer Within—A Practitioner's*

*Introduction to Therapeutic Touch* and *Psychoimmunity and the Healing Process,* which promises that we can unite our mind and body and "access our own innate abilities to achieve health and balance in our lives." The list is endless.

Of course we all agree that the mind has a great influence over the body; the two work together in ways we do not fully understand. The error of "holistic health" is that the mind is given supernatural powers; the assumption is that *you can be your own healer because you can be your own god.* One devotee claimed that "unseen doctors are working through me." The witch doctor is back, but this time he holds expensive seminars and has a "scientific" explanation for his occult powers.

A man who was healed of a serious disease in a so-called healing meeting discovered he inherited a "demonic darkness," that is, a persistent sense that an evil presence was nearby. When he rebuked Satan, the emotional and spiritual cloud left him, but his disease returned. We should not be surprised that healings occur in all the religions of the world. Satan is willing to do some "good" in exchange for blind allegiance.

## Psychedelic Drugs and Transcendental Meditation

In her book *The Aquarian Conspiracy,* Marilyn Ferguson predicted that a "paradigm shift" is taking place in the West. We are leaving the world of logic and reason and appealing to the world of imagination and feeling. "We are not victims or pawns . . . we control," she writes.[9] We are now left in charge of ourselves. Human nature is neither good nor bad, but what we need is a spiritual experience— and that is through the emptying of the mind of all conscious thought by means of meditation. She says psychedelic drugs speed up the process. Meditation and drugs used together empty the mind and immobilize the will.

On the surface, practices such as transcendental meditation appear harmless. What could possibly be wrong with spending time trying to empty the mind of all the pressures of life and just think about *nothing?* Combine that with exercise that demands concentration, and your blood pressure is sure to drop and your finely tuned body will feel much better.

But transcendental meditation is based on the religious conviction that that the soul must be united with the one unified force of the universe. Rationality is seen as the hindrance to this oneness and mystical unity with God. As long as I am thinking about something, I perceive myself to be distinct from the objects of this world. Thus, I must empty my mind of specific thoughts and try to think of contentless reality. S. N. Dasgupta writes that the yogi "steadily proceeds toward that ultimate state in which his mind will be disintegrated and his self will shine forth in its own light and he himself will be absolutely free in bondless, companionless loneliness of self-illumination."[10]

At some point, the participant experiences a conversion experience called enlightenment. This mystical experience enables one to go beyond personality, morality, and knowledge. The conversion Satan has wrought is complete—the transformation of consciousness has occurred. But with demonic spirits influencing the mind, there is a cloud of darkness rather than enlightenment that enters the soul. This deception can only be uncovered in honest contemplation in the presence of God, Bible in hand.

## In Touch with Your Angel

There is an overbelief in angels in our society. As of this writing, Hollywood has produced at least three dozen films, made-for-TV movies, and series featuring heavenly beings. Angel stores have sprung up in Los Angeles and New York. All of this is based on the happy assumption that angels are about us, waiting to help anyone who is in distress, regardless of his or her religious convictions or lifestyle. In every episode of the TV series Touched by an Angel, a troubled person is helped; either there is a dramatic rescue or healing, or some helpful intervention. Whatever, an angel is used by God to resolve the crisis, proving that there is a spiritual dimension to the world and that the Almighty stands ready to help us by sending an angel to those who least deserve or expect it.

Since angels seem more approachable than God, it is not surprising that people are drawn to these beings. If we make contact with them, we will not have to face the holiness of God; angels are believed to be more sympathetic to us, more just like we are. Our problem is not sin; it is disconnectedness that angels can help us overcome.

Obviously, this view of angels is loaded with theology, a cultural theology that reinforces prevalent views about man and God. We are not seen as sinners standing helplessly before God and needing the protection of the righteousness of Christ. What is more, it assumes that all angels are good; indeed, God is good, angels are good, and all is right in the world. Or, at least, the angels are here to help it become right.

Keep in mind that the Bible teaches that there are two different kinds of angels. Those who serve God have a specific task; they are "ministering spirits sent to serve those who will inherit salvation" (Hebrews 1:14). As far as I know, every time good angels are mentioned in Scripture in relationship to the unconverted, it is always in judgment. We think of the angels who executed judgment on Sodom and Gomorrah. They helped Lot escape, but only because he was a believer in Jehovah and therefore a "righteous man" (2 Peter 2:7). Repeatedly in the book of Revelation, angels are executing judgment on a Christ-rejecting world (e.g., 14:10).

As for evil angels, they duplicate, whenever possible, the miracles of Christ. Paul warned that Satan would come with "counterfeit miracles, signs and wonders" (2 Thessalonians 2:9). Evil angels will do helpful miracles if they can and if it serves their purpose: diverting people from the purity of the gospel of Christ. We must rebuke the grand lie that anyone can come to God in any way, without a mediator, without a sacrifice.

Yes, even "angels" can be one more route into the occult. More than one person has discovered that "helpful" angels can turn out to be spirits who seek more and more control; spirits under the direction of Lucifer, the chief of the fallen angels.

## Hard Rock and "Free" Sex

"Of course Rock and sex go together," a participant at the more recent Woodstock event of 1999 said when a commentator asked about the nudity and open sexuality tolerated at the gathering. "Yes, of course, Rock, reflecting rebellion, and immorality, with its hedonistic 'selfism,' are inseparable." The reason for the loud music is so that mind and heart might be totally captivated and that the noise will drown out the voice of conscience.

Five themes are repeated in rock music: (1) sex, (2) drugs, (3) rebellion, (4) false religion, and (5) Satan. Rock music is intended to break down any resistance to immorality and indecency. As Mick Jagger said, "We've had their bodies . . . now we want their minds." Little wonder that those who participate in that lifestyle are open to overt demonic activity. They are living in the devil's playpen, enjoying the devil's toys.

How serious is rebellion? To King Saul, who did things "his way," God said through Samuel, "For rebellion is like the sin of divination, and arrogance like the evil of idolatry" (1 Samuel 15:23). Rebellion is connected to divination, and arrogance is like idolatry.

There are various levels of demonic influence in the lives of those who dabble in the occult. Some might experience occasional demonic influence and harassment; others might experience demonic visitations or the persistent sense that evil spirits are nearby. Others might actually be demon possessed. In *People of the Lie,* M. Scott Peck observed that "it seems clear from the literature on possession that a majority of cases have had involvement with the occult—a frequency far greater than might be expected in the general population."[11]

Enough said.

## THE DEPTHS OF THE DARKNESS

We've learned that teenagers are targeted for Satan's most deceptive lies, with multiple opportunities to enter the diverse and luring world of the occult. One snare after another is carefully set before them through entertainment, video games, and books. Not only is it seductive, but it also appears to be fun. Many have no idea that they are entering Satan's territory through the *Satanic Bible,* fantasy games (such as Dungeons and Dragons), drugs, heavy metal music, and seances. Many teenagers are empty and searching. As one of them said, "I was so open and so vulnerable to receive anything that would fill me up, you know, make me feel like a valuable person. So I was open to receive whatever the devil would give me. Or God, or whatever . . . it didn't matter to me."

We can understand the desperation of children brought up in homes where there is alcoholism, abuse, or loneliness. Hollywood preys on their emptiness and draws them into a world that has fascination and intrigue. They watch occult movies, not realizing that these shows are an open invitation for satanic involvement and deception. The teenagers are looking for a thrill, and as they delve into the occult world they begin to wonder what it would be like to kill an animal or prick one's finger and drink his or her own blood.

We've already learned that witchcraft of various sorts is made appealing to young people. Some of these teenagers then progress to self-styled groups, such as a coven. Teens are often recruited into these through free drugs and uninhibited sex. They are lured by the open sexuality of these rituals; they are assured that nothing is too degrading, nothing is *not* permissible. Often at the coven, a nude woman lies on top of the altar. During sex orgies, which are the hallmark of satanic worship, the participants are often secretly videotaped and then blackmailed if they want to leave the group.

The telltale signs of direct satanic ritualism are the mutilation of animals, unbridled sexuality, and, in brief, the compulsion to want to go over the edge and do anything. Magic gives way to incredulity, for the victim may be taught that if you torture an animal you amplify its life force, thereby absorbing its personal power. The teen is assured that he belongs to a highly select group, and he must remain loyal to his commitment. Some make a pact with the devil, signed in their own blood.

Of course witchcraft is anxious to portray its "good" side. In a news article called "Witchcraft Gets Army's Blessing," Mike Drago reports that at Fort Hood, Texas, and four other army bases, soldiers who practice the ancient wiccan faith have now received the army's blessing. Those willing to listen heard a lecture stating that witchcraft believes "in the divinity of all things" and holds that we are "all of one life force" and the human race is "one with nature." Though originally apprehensive, the army has now sanctioned such groups.[12]

To be fair, we must point out that not all witches directly worship Satan. Some are opposed to animal sacrifices because they see everything in nature as divine. These witches attempt to be in harmony with nature, developing their hidden psychic power. But whether Satan is worshiped directly or under the guise of nature, the end result is essentially the same. There are only two personal spiritual powers in the universe, God and the devil.

There are also hard-core satanists, found internationally throughout the world. They kill, abduct, and brainwash, always in secret. There are perhaps between forty to sixty thousand people killed in the world each year in ritual homicides. Dr. Al Carlisle of the Utah State Prison System has estimated that in metropolitan areas hundreds of persons meet their deaths in satanic ceremonies each year![13] In cahoots with the devil, young women are used as breeders to furnish babies that are used in ritual abuse, worship of Satan, and murder. The police tell us that we are in a new era of "ritualistic-oriented crime" in our nation and also in other countries. Yes, such crimes happen all over the world.

What promises does Satan make that invite the curious to begin those first steps that for many lead to such wanton evil? There is the lure of power, the supposed ability to effect curses over others, the right to punish and reward as one wills. In effect, the devil offers his prey the right to play god that he might be worshiped even as God is worshiped. Though Satan makes the same promises as God, he, of necessity, cannot keep his word. He is as far from God as one can travel.

What follows is a sketch of the way to freedom, the indispensable principles that will set people free. Obviously, there can be no freedom unless a power greater than Satan comes to take control.

## THE WAY TO FREEDOM

Satan's greatest fear is that we will understand that he is defeated and that God has made it possible to send him from us. He fears detection and bold confrontation. If we truly believed that all sin was our enemy and never our friend; if we kept ourselves free of satanic involvement, we would be able to flee Satan.

To resist him, there must be both a defense and an offense.

Warning: Let's never forget that the best defense against the occult is to refuse every invitation to become involved in its many overtures. Again: ask any army general and he will tell you that it is always easier to defend territory than to win it back after it has been conceded to the enemy. Those of us who have children must warn them of the danger of dabbling in what God has specifically forbidden.

We must always see sin as our enemy, never as our friend. When faced with a moral or spiritual choice, we often think we can sin without serious consequences. We must remember that when we tolerate sin, we also tolerate the devil. Sin is his playground, his trap.

Of course there is hope for those who have been involved in some aspect of occult activity. If you believe that Satan will retaliate as you seek to be free of occult activity, I encourage you to be absolutely convinced about the triumph of Christ over all evil spirits. Keep in mind that on the cross Christ won a decisive victory; the serpent has already been crushed. "He forgave us all our sins, having canceled the written code, with its regulations, that was against us and that stood opposed to us; he took it away, nailing it to the cross. And having disarmed the powers and authorities, he made a public spectacle of them, triumphing over them by the cross" (Colossians 2:13–15). Only when looking at Christ will we not be intimidated, for *Satan has as much power as God lets him have and not one whit more.*

We do not fight from the standpoint of weakness or doubt; we fight from the solid rock of victory and faith in a triumphant Christ. But I must clarify that getting free from satanic power is not just a once-for-all act but rather a lifestyle. Also, the steps listed below might have to be repeated; one act of renunciation, one decisive moment of repentance, is not sufficient. Depending on the level and kind of involvement, it is possible that you need counseling to help you break the bonds that hold you to the dark side of the spirit world.

Now for some help.

1. *You must repent of your involvement with false, occult religion.* Take the time to list the different kinds of occult involvement; you might want to check a list of occult techniques and practices. Many people who think they have participated in only one form of occultism upon reflection remember involvement in other related sins.

At Moody Church, where I serve, a minister gave a powerful message on the occult and listed forty different entry points or practices that lead to such enslavement. That evening, he invited all those who had some form of involvement and wanted freedom to stay behind for counsel. About thirty-five people stayed for counsel, and incredibly all forty of the occult techniques were represented (many of the people were, of course, involved in more than one form of occult activity).

Repent of this involvement, asking God to break the ties that still bind. For example, a prayer might be, "Father, I thank You that I belong to You; You have 'delivered me from the power of darkness and translated me into the kingdom of Your dear Son' [see Colossians 1:13 KJV], and I claim that transfer of authority and privilege. I renounce my involvement in _____ and break all ties to this evil. I affirm that I am 'in Christ' and therefore am no longer subject to Satan and his kingdom. Today I thank You for the victory Christ purchased for me. I affirm the power of the Cross and the Resurrection as belonging to me."

*2. Identify the lie that led you into Satan's trap.* Try to answer the question of how he tried to take God's place: Did you seek occult power, knowledge, or an experience that promised to give meaning to your life? Or perhaps you believed the lie that it is possible to approach God in many different ways; or you thought that God was simply whatever you wanted Him to be.

To rectify the lie, read and memorize passages of Scripture that contradict the false teaching. For example, it is Christ who came to give us fulfillment, not Satan, and there can only be one way to God (John 10:10; 14:6). Since Satan often strikes a blow to our self-worth, read passages that speak of our glorious position of being "in Christ" (e.g., Colossians 3:1–3).

*3. Burn all bridges—all of the entry points to the occult must be left behind.* Be sure to get rid of all artifacts and articles, whether they be Ouija boards, horoscope books, or violent games and the like. You must be held accountable to stay away from all people and places that led you into occult sin. This is more difficult than it seems, particularly if you live with those who are prone to influence you to return to the pagan practices. We have this promise: "Submit yourselves, then, to God. Resist the devil, and he will flee from you" (James 4:7). There is great power in the name of Christ, but only for those who are submissive to His authority.

*4. As far as possible have your relationships with others "above reproach."*

If someone has wronged you, you must lay down all bitterness, giving it over to God, entrusting your wounded sense of justice to Him. "If you forgive anyone, I also forgive him. And what I have forgiven—if there was anything to forgive—I have forgiven in the sight of Christ for your sake, in order that Satan might not outwit us. For we are not unaware of his schemes" (2 Corinthians 2:10–11). Satan uses ruptured human relationships as a launching pad.

5. *Submit to human authority within the body of Christ, that is, the church.* Jesus, you will recall, chided His disciples as to why they could not cast out a demon by saying, "This kind does not go out except by prayer and fasting" (Matthew 17:21, margin; cf. Mark 9:29). Strongholds given over to Satan are sometimes not easily recaptured, and there is strength in numbers. We can't climb out of some pits on our own.

You need the strength of the body of Christ for mutual help and accountability. No, we cannot win our battles alone. In Ephesians 6, Paul lists various pieces of armor needed in our fight against spiritual powers. After saying that our feet should be "shod with the gospel of peace," he says, "In addition to all this, take up the shield of faith, with which you can extinguish all the flaming arrows of the evil one" (Ephesians 6:16). In ancient times shields were beveled, so that they could be interlocked. As the army marched, they formed a moving wall that opposing soldiers found difficult to penetrate. Just so, as those in Satan's grip lock arms with other believers, they will discover that, yes, there is a way out of the traps the Enemy has set.

Yes, Satan hates us and has a destructive plan for our lives, but we can make sure it is not fulfilled. Let us make sure that it exists only as a dream in his darkened mind. We have the promise "Greater is he that is in you, than he that is in the world" (1 John 4:4 KJV).

## A PRAYER TO BEGIN THE JOURNEY

*Father, I thank You today that Satan was defeated*
*by Christ on the cross. I thank You that the serpent's*
*head was crushed in the dust, as You predicted. Today I*

*affirm that I can live differently; I thank You that victory was purchased for me by Christ's resurrection and ascension into heaven, where He is seated "far above all rule and authority, power and dominion, and every title that can be given, not only in the present age but also in the one to come" (Ephesians 1:20–21), and I thank You that I am seated there with Him. Grant me the grace to apply His promises against Satan and his hordes. I hereby serve Satan notice that his days over me have come to an end. Help me to take the steps needed to walk before You in freedom and fellowship.*

*I pray this in the worthy and powerful name of Jesus, my conquering Lord. Amen.*

# ENLISTING GOD'S SPECIAL HELP

*S*eneca cried, "O that a hand would come down from heaven and deliver me of my besetting sin." In Jesus he received his wish.

If you have read these pages and still feel that something might be missing in your life, let me take a moment to explain how you can have the assurance that you belong to God—the God who will be with you through your personal struggles, disappointments, and triumphs. Perhaps the basis of your relationship with the Almighty is still on a shaky foundation. And perhaps you must be reminded of the reason we can break with a sinful lifestyle.

Keep in mind that when Jesus Christ died on the cross, His death was a sacrifice for us as sinners. "For Christ died for sins once for all, the righteous for the unrighteous, to bring you to God" (1 Peter 3:18). As a result, we can be accepted by God on the basis of Christ's merit; we are received by God even as His Beloved is received. Our part is to admit to our sinfulness and transfer all of our trust to Christ; only then is His righteousness credited to our account. If you believe that Jesus did all that ever will be necessary for you to stand in

God's presence and you embrace His work for yourself, you will be saved and know it. This is known as justification by faith alone, through grace alone, because of Christ alone.

However, the message of the Cross extends beyond our obvious need for acceptance and forgiveness. Christ died not only that we might be forgiven, but also that we might be delivered from the power of sin. The same Cross that purchased our salvation purchased our deliverance.

Specifically, this means that believers have been identified with Christ in His redeeming work on earth. "But because of his great love for us, God, who is rich in mercy, made us alive with Christ even when we were dead in transgressions—it is by grace you have been saved. And God raised us up with Christ and seated us with him in the heavenly realms in Christ Jesus" (Ephesians 2:4–6). The phrases "made us alive," "raised us up," and "seated us" are all successive historical events in the saving career of Jesus. Yet, interestingly, Paul is not writing about Jesus, but about us!

This union with Christ is the basis for transforming our lifestyle and desires. Despite our struggles and failures, we must not think of ourselves as sinners or as addicts but rather as redeemed people joined to Christ for a life of spiritual freedom and personal holiness. If we can keep in mind who we actually are—that is, as being "in Christ"—we can withstand the attacks of temptation more easily. We will see ourselves as those who no longer need to obey the desires of the flesh, for we have a new relationship and spiritual identity.

Paul explicitly bases our spiritual freedom on this union with Christ. "If we have been united with him like this in his death, we will certainly also be united with him in his resurrection. For we know that our old self was crucified with him so that the body of sin might be done away with, that we should no longer be slaves to sin—because anyone who has died has been freed from sin" (Romans 6:5–7).

This leads us to several principles that will help us in overcoming the powerful urges of temptation and fleshly conduct.

First, *the triumph of Christ over sin and the devil is completed and thorough.* Satan is unable to bring an attack against us unless God allows him to do so. Temptation of any kind cannot assault us unless

God permits it; indeed, the whole spiritual realm is subject to Christ, who is seated "far above all rule and authority, power and dominion, and every title that can be given, not only in the present age but also in the one to come" (Ephesians 1:20–21). The better we see the undisputed nature of Christ's triumph the more eager we will be to look to Him for the deliverance we so desperately need.

Why does Jesus, who has infinite power, not protect us by stopping the devil and subduing our desires? The answer is that the world, the flesh, and the devil are given to us that we might fight against them and win; in a word, the more intense the struggle the greater the victory and joy in overcoming the power of sin. Believe it or not, God wants to increase our joy and give us the opportunity to "receive a rich welcome into the eternal kingdom of our Lord and Savior Jesus Christ" (2 Peter 1:11).

Second, *everything God asks us to do is based on what Christ has already done.* Are we asked to say no to fleshly desires? Yes, we are, but it is because we can count ourselves "dead to sin but alive to God in Christ Jesus. Therefore do not let sin reign in your mortal body so that you obey its evil desires" (Romans 6:11–12). We subdue the fleshly conduct because Jesus broke sin's power.

If we ask the question of why we continue to fail even though we are "joined to Christ," the answer is that Paul's words refer to our position and authority but must be applied to our experience. By no means is this union with Christ merely theoretical; it is real and actual but cannot be taken for granted.

Years ago a woman sought my advice: she was living with a man, but wanted out of the relationship. I suggested she move out, but the matter was not quite that simple. They were living in her apartment. She asked her live-in companion to leave, but he threatened that he would "get even." He argued he had a right to live in her apartment since they had been together for more than a year.

What should she do? She took my suggestion and filed a police report and got a court order that he be evicted. He ranted and raved, but finally he left in a huff. Soon after this she changed the locks on the doors, and to my knowledge she has not seen him since. But what gave this 115-pound woman the courage to evict a man who was twice her strength and perhaps three times her weight? The law was on her side. And in the final analysis, the man had no rights to the apartment, no matter how loudly he protested.

We also have the right to evict the devil and avoid his subtle snares. Of course he will not leave peacefully. He will argue, intimidate us, and continue to try to have us believe a lie. So the fact that Christ was victorious does not mean we will be; it means that we have the potential to be extricated from the entanglements that sin brings.

Third, *since faith is critical to have our inner lives transformed, we must realize that only a life of renewed obedience will help us avoid a repeat of past performances.* I wish I could give you a formula that would guarantee that your repentance was final, complete, and long-lasting. I cannot. I can, however, assure you that the spiritual disciplines—Scripture mediation, prayer, and the fellowship of other believers—are all helpful, if not necessary, in winning the war.

At all costs, never give up in your personal struggles. God comes to the aid of those who need His help the most. "The Lord is near to all who call on him, to all who call on him in truth" (Psalm 145:18). Name your struggle, your particular sin, and I will assure you that somewhere there is someone with the same temptation who has overcome his or her past and now walks confidently with God.

I leave you with this word of assurance: "His divine power has given us everything we need for life and godliness through our knowledge of him who called us by his own glory and goodness. Through these he has given us his very great and precious promises, so that through them you may participate in the divine nature and escape the corruption in the world caused by evil desires" (2 Peter 1:3–4)

God can both keep us from Satan's snares and deliver us out of them if we are ready to respond to His grace. He is ready. Are we?

# NOTES

## Introduction: Welcome to the War

1. Wayne Stiles, "Things Are Not Always As They Seem," *Kindred Spirit,* Autumn 1999, 16.

2. Quoted in Warren W. Wiersbe, *Preaching and Teaching with Imagination* (Wheaton, Ill.: Scripture Press, Victor Books, 1994), 64.

3. Quoted in Spiros Zodhiates, *The Behavior of Belief* (Grand Rapids: Eerdmans, 1966), 236.

## Snare #1: Greed: The Heart Revealed

1. Michael Douglas, as Gordon Gekko, in *Wall Street,* writ. Stanley Weiser and Oliver Stone; dir., Oliver Stone, 125 min. (original), Twentieth Century Fox and Entertainment Producers, 1987 (film), 1996 (videocassette); videocassette.

2. Howard Clinebell, *Understanding and Counseling Persons with Alcohol, Drug and Behavioral Addictions* (Nashville: Abingdon, 1984), 128.

3. *The World Book Dictionary,* A–K (Chicago: Scott Fetzer, 1985), 708.

4. Bruce Knecht and Jeffrey Taylor, "SEC Charges New Era, Bennett Defrauded Charities, Big Investors," *The Wall Street Journal,* 22 May 1995, A1.

## Snare #2: Gambling: Is It a Good Bet?

1. Rex M. Rogers, *Seducing America: Is Gambling a Good Bet?* (Grand Rapids: Baker, 1997), 16.

2. James Dobson, *Family News,* April 1999, 1.

3. Ibid.

4. Shirley Barnes, "Betting Their Way into a Burden of Debt," *Chicago Tribune,* 29 August 1999, 13.

5. Johnny Greene, "The Gambling Trap," *Psychology Today,* September 1982, 55.

6. "In Detroit, Cop's Suicide Casts a Pall over Casinos," *Chicago Tribune,* 28 January 2000, 24.

7. Joe Atkins, "The States' Bad Bet," *Christianity Today,* 25 November 1991, 20.

8. John W. Kennedy, "Gambling Away the Golden Years," *Christianity Today,* 24 May 1999, 54.

9. Arnie Wexler, quoted in Rogers, *Seducing America,* 102.

10. Rogers, *Seducing America,* 66.

11. Ibid., 64.

12. Barnes, "Betting Their Way into a Burden of Debt," 5.

## Snare #3: Alcoholism: Quitting Tomorrow

1. Craig Nakken, *The Addictive Personality* (Center City, Minn.: Hazelden, 1988), 35. I'm indebted to this helpful book for many of the ideas shared in this chapter.

2. Quoted in John Bradshaw, *Healing the Shame That Binds You* (Deerfield Beach, Fla.: Health Communications, 1988), 95. This book has many helpful insights but fails to make a distinction between objective shame before God and the shame that has been communicated to us by bad parenting or personal misconceptions.

3. Nakken, *The Addictive Personality,* 35.

4. Robert Louis Stevenson, *Dr. Jekyll and Mr. Hyde* (New York: Pollard & Moses, 1888), 67.

5. Jerry G. Dunn, *God Is for the Alcoholic* (Chicago: Moody, 1975), 53.

6. Interview with William Raws, The Addiction Recovery Center, America's Keswick, Whiting, New Jersey.

7. Bradshaw, *Healing the Shame That Binds You* (Deerfield Beach, Fla.: Health Communications, 1993), 10.

8. Ibid., 12.

## Snare #4: Pornography: The Soul Defiled

1. *American Family Journal,* April 1999, 21.

2. Charles Swindoll, quoted in Henry J. Rogers, *The Silent War: Ministering to Those Trapped in the Deception of Pornography* (Green Forest, Ark.: New Leaf, 2000), 54.

3. Laurie Hall, *An Affair of the Mind: One Woman's Courageous Battle to Salvage Her Family from the Devastation of Pornography* (Colorado Springs: Focus on the Family, 1996), quoted in "Impact, Coral Ridge Ministries," October 1996, 2.

4. William Barclay, *The Gospel of Matthew,* vol. 1, The Daily Study Bible Series (Edinburgh: St. Andrew, 1956), 145.

5. Benjamin Needler, in *Puritan Sermons,* 1659–1689, vol. 1, ed. Samuel Annesley and James Nichols (reprint; Wheaton, Ill.: Richard Owen Roberts, 1981), 53.

6. Walter Trobisch, *Love Is a Feeling to Be Learned* (pamphlet; Downers Grove, Ill.: Inter-Varsity, 1971, 1974), 18.

## Snare #5: The Sexual Affair: A Poisoned Oasis

1. Name Withheld, "The Subtlety of Sexual Sin" *Eternity,* February 1977, 28.

2. Charles Mylander, *Running the Red Lights: Putting the Brakes on Sexual Temptation* (Ventura, Calif.: Regal, 1986), 19.

3. Michael Castleman, "Addicted to Love," *Chicago Tribune,* Style, 30 January 1991, 6.

4. Patrick Carnes, *Out of the Shadows* (Minneapolis: CompCare, 1983), ix. This is a helpful book for understanding the mind and struggles of an addict; here, at last, we see the shadowy world into which he retreats. The book, however, does not address the important issue of God's forgiveness and the power of Christian conversion.

5. Ibid.

6. David Carter, *Torn Asunder: Recovering from Extramarital Affairs* (Chicago: Moody, 1992).

## Snare #6: The Search for Pleasure: Running on Empty

1. Blaise Pascal, *The Mind on Fire: An Anthology of the Writings of Blaise Pascal,* ed. James Houston (Portland: Multnomah, 1989), 108–9.

2. Neil Postman, *Amusing Ourselves to Death* (New York: Viking Penguin, 1985), 3–4.

3. Ibid., 87.

4. Ibid., 104.

5. Sabrina L. Miller, "Sand, Sun, Suds Meet Scripture on Spring Break," *Chicago Tribune,* 2 April 2000, 1.

6. Stephen R. Covey, *First Things First* (New York: Rockefeller Center, 1994), 28.

7. Rodney Clapp, "Why the Devil Takes Visa," *Christianity Today,* 7 October 1966, 20–21.

8. Ibid., 20.

9. Ibid.

10. John Piper, *The Pleasures of God* (Portland: Multnomah, 1991), 88.

11. Peter Marshall, quoted in *Christianity Today,* 10 August 1998, 72.

12. Richard Roper, "'Yes' Earns 15 Minutes of Martyrdom," *Chicago Sun Times,* 10 June 1999, 3.

13. Henri Nouwen, *The Way of the Heart* (San Francisco: Harper, 1981), 21.

14. Clapp, "Why the Devil Takes Visa," 32.

## Snare #7: Occultism: Superstition or Deception?

1. Margaret Kim Peterson, "Weird Sisters," *Books and Culture: A Christian Review,* March/April 1999, 24.

2. Ibid., 25

3. Ibid.

4. Ibid.

5. Ibid.

6. Ibid.

7. Ibid.

8. Anton LaVey, quoted in John Ankerberg and John Weldon, *The Coming Darkness* (Eugene, Ore: Harvest House, 1993), 94.

9. Marilyn Ferguson, *The Aquarian Conspiracy* (Los Angeles: Jeremy P. Tarcher, 1980), 104.

10. S. N. Dasgupta, *Hindu Mysticism* (New York: Frederick Unger, 1927), 79.

11. M. Scott Peck, *People of the Lie,* in Ankerberg and Weldon, *The Coming Darkness,* 66.

12. Mike Drago, "Witchcraft Gets Army's Blessing," *Chicago Tribune,* 18 June 1999.

13. Jerry Johnson, *The Edge of Evil: The Rise of Satanism in North America* (Waco, Tex.: Word, 1989), 4.

Moody Press, a ministry of Moody Bible Institute,
is designed for education, evangelization, and edification.
If we may assist you in knowing more about Christ
and the Christian life, please write us without obligation:
Moody Press, c/o MLM, Chicago, Illinois 60610.